Song of Thunder

by the same author

THE IDES OF APRIL
SWORD SLEEP
BEYOND THE DESERT GATE

A TENT FOR THE SUN

LIVING IN EARLIEST GREECE

STANDING LIONS

Song of Thunder

Mary Ray

Faber and Faber
London · Boston

First published in 1978
by Faber and Faber Limited
3 Queen Square London WC1
Reprinted 1978
Printed and bound in Great Britain by
Redwood Burn Ltd Trowbridge and Esher

© *Mary Ray 1978*

British Library Cataloguing in Publication Data

Ray, Mary
    Song of thunder.
I. Title
823'.9'1J   PZ7.R21015

ISBN 0-571-11160-2

Contents

Foreword

The people who lived there called the island Kallisté, "the beautiful one", for it must indeed have been beautiful, rising to a central cluster of peaks from a sea shaded with colours like a peacock's feather, and rich with orchards and vineyards. It lay far out in the Aegean Sea, south from the main scattering of islands; when the sailors of Kallisté looked out from their harbour the sea was empty round the whole circle of their horizon. Even Crete, the Great Island, was far away to the south. Kallisté was prosperous; perhaps her people had been colonists and traders from the ancient kingdoms of Crete. While they grew rich and adorned their homes they did not know that the fate of their island was to be a strange and terrible one, spreading—when it came—far beyond the circle of their empty horizon.

Yet Kallisté has now lived three different lives. The first ended perhaps about 1450 B.C. At the beginning of the classical period Dorians like those who conquered Sparta came there and called the island Thera. Now, if you look for it on a map, you will find the name Santorini, and the island is once again beautiful, but in a way that those who knew it first would find hard to recognise.

The name "Kallisté" has three syllables, and I have added an accent to make this clear.

PART ONE
Kallisté

1 § The Master

Kenofer came out through the gateway of the governor's palace and stood, screwing up his eyes against the brilliant light. He was looking out over the town and the harbour below, but he saw nothing. He had not trusted his voice even to greet the guard, who had known his father; the strain of walking out quietly and not running like a punished child was as much as he could manage for the moment. And Phormio would be waiting for him one turn below on the path; he wasn't ready even for him.

He walked to the far side of the platform outside the gate and stood under the umbrella pine which gave some shade to the guard. The palace was built on the eastern headland above the shallow bay that passed for a harbour here on Kallisté, and the rock went down almost sheer to a stretch of water iridescent as a peacock's feather, lapis and turquoise-colour over patches of sand. Further out it shelved suddenly deep and the water went dark. He seemed to be studying the small ledges with their tufts of yellow vetch and bleached grasses, but he was still seeing nothing.

The guard watched him, knowing part of it and guessing the rest from the way Kenofer was standing, stiffly, but with his shoulders drooping. He saw a slim boy, his bare body tanned very brown above his best red kilt, long hair knotted back to the crown of his head as if he were dressed for a festival; he looked like a hundred boys on the island except for the lyre in its leather case hanging across his shoulders. The Lord Aglauros, the Governor, was a man of refined tastes and clearly he had been practising his famous wit at the expense of the son of his former fresco painter.

There was the sound of footsteps coming up the path from the town below and the guard straightened into his duty position. He knew that Kenofer had too much sense to jump from the cliff, and he would have put the lyre down first anyway.

Phormio had seen his friend from below and come up for him. Taller, and thickset for an islander, with lighter hair, he looked the older of the two, but they had been born within a month of each other. Like the guard he did not need to be told what had happened.

"You're here, then?"

Kenofer looked towards him and managed a shrug but no words.

"Coming?"

Kenofer raised a hand in salute to the guard and led the way down towards the town. Phormio followed a little behind, his own face bleak now. There was nothing he could say to help; Kenofer was the one who was good with words.

Above the first houses Kenofer stopped and turned and then Phormio could put an arm round his shoulders and lead him out of the hard white light to the outcrop of rock under the fig-tree which was one of the resting-places for people climbing uphill from the town.

"They'll be waiting at home and I've got to tell them. Oh Phormio!"

Kenofer's voice was flat and bleak. Automatically he unslung the lyre and set it between his knees, smoothing the glowing polish on the dark wood with long strong fingers which were broad at the tips, as if he got comfort simply from the touch.

"Tell me first, for practice."

"I asked to see the Governor, he kept me waiting a long time. You know that, you were waiting too." It came out like something he was learning by heart.

"I know, I hoped it meant something good."

"It didn't. I think someone had told Aglauros why I had come and he wanted time to polish what he was going to say."

"What did he say?"

"Well, he sat there and I stood—it was on the south terrace. I was surprised when they took me there, it's in the private part of the palace. Then I understood. Do you remember the fresco that everyone talked about, the last one? It was painted in the arcade of the south terrace?"

"The one with dolphins?"

"Dolphins and flying fish, it was supposed to be his best, before . . ." Before the fever, Phormio added in his mind. "All the time I was speaking, I could see a man whitewashing the wall behind Aglauros's head, as if the dolphins were drowning one after the other in white mud." He took a breath and then started again.

"I said what we'd planned. That the God had given me some skill with the lyre and that I would be honoured if in serving him I could develop the gift I have been given. He knows, Aglauros knows everything, that old Dymas can't teach me anything now. What I need is to practise and to listen. The best bards north of the Great Island come to Kallisté; he's known for his taste."

"And he said no? You knew he might."

"I suppose so. Yes, I did. I knew, only I didn't believe it. I hadn't looked further than his saying yes."

"What did he say?"

"Nothing at first, he just looked. You know how his eyes are close together but deep-set so you can't see into them. He looked, no glanced, half over his shoulder, and then he said, 'Yes, you do take after your father,' and then, 'Show me what you can do.' And I thought at least he was giving me a chance.

I got my lyre out and looked round for somewhere to sit. There was a stool on the edge of the terrace but as I went towards it he said 'Who gave you leave to sit in my presence?' "

"But how could you play then?" Phormio turned towards his friend in horror and saw that he was shaking, his hands gripping the sides of the lyre.

"I shouldn't have. I should have gone then, but I couldn't believe it. I started to play as well as I could, you know, the song I said I would if there was a chance. But the lyre slipped and I played a wrong note, just one. He stopped me then with two raised fingers, as if he was calling a slave, and said 'Kenofer, son of Megaros, my terrace is no place for you to practise what you call your art, any more than it was for your father.' And while I stood there not understanding he called the steward and said to him across me, as if I wasn't there, 'This brat is not to be admitted again, for any reason, ever,' and then he turned away."

Kenofer swung round then, his hands trembling so that the lyre strings hummed in protest. "Phormio, what am I to do? It's there in me, I know. I have to learn to play better and he's stopping me. Wiping it all out, the way he's having Father's picture painted out."

They stood up together and Phormio put out a hand again towards his friend, but Kenofer shrugged it away.

"No . . . Oh go away please. Don't you see? I've still got to tell Mother."

Phormio said, "Not about the painting!"

Kenofer turned back after three steps. "No, not about the painting, or what he said. Just the 'no' will be enough, don't you think?"

He ran down the steep path between the first of the houses. Phormio watched him, standing with his large hands useless at his sides. Feeling hurt and yet knowing it had no more been meant than the snap of a cur in pain when a man tries to find a thorn in its pad. He turned away from the main path and went down towards the harbour by a steeper and narrower way.

Kenofer stopped running at the corner above his house. His mother and small sister would both be there. His mother, whose month it was for duty at the shrine of the Mistress, tired but waiting proudly for good news. Theano, who still cried for her father in her sleep, would be sitting arranging and rearranging her small clay dolls in their little house, her eyes large in a small pale face. No, it was too soon to tell them yet.

He had not thought where he would go, but his feet took him downhill, down the steep steps that led to the harbour. He lived high on the hill above the town where the larger houses caught the breeze, but further down the walls leaned closer together, and there was the harbour smell of fishheads and hot stone and donkey-droppings.

Ahead water dazzled above the low sheds of the boat-builders and there was the regular background clatter of adze strokes and sawing. He knew all the island boats drawn up on the shingle beach: a broad-bellied trading galley from Amnissos, harbour of the Great Island, that was loading last season's wine, lay beside a lean scout boat from the High King's sea patrol that had broken a steering oar. Workmen were swarming over her, fitting a new one. The strong wind that had not completely died down from the summer storm of the night before tugged at their kilts and long hair.

Kenofer climbed the breakwater. A fisherman, working on his net, stood up in the high prow of his boat, shouted to the workmen and pointed. Kenofer turned to look the same way; a boat was rounding the west headland, where it rose sheer above the sea. Even from so far away he could see there was something wrong with her, the top third of her mast lost and a clutter of spars and rigging trailing over the side. She wallowed in the strong current that set round the point, listing almost out of control with a torn fragment of her sail lashed to give the steersman a little way to try to bring her across to the harbour beach.

A sailor's child with red hair was scrambling over the wet rocks below the breakwater.

"Look, she's from Melos!" His eyes were keener than Kenofer's, and could already decipher the pattern of once bright paint flaking from her bow.

Kenofer squatted down to talk to the child.

"Would she have been caught in the blow last night?"

"Seems like it. It came up sudden, but it does at midsummer."

"She must have been in a hurry, to chance it. I wonder why?"

The child crunched away across the shingle to be there when the boat beached, but Kenofer stayed where he was on the breakwater. He was expecting no news from Melos, a night and a day's sail away to the north-west.

A crowd had gathered to shout and help and draw her up the beach. Kenofer watched a man carried up into the town; he must have been injured when the gear came down. Then there were others, three passengers trailing up towards the houses, bedraggled and uncertain on their feet. One was a man walking alone, a sailor behind carrying his baggage; but before he disappeared between the builder's sheds there was a flash of polished metal and of the red kilts of the Governor's guard clattering down steps that led directly to the harbour from the palace.

The man turned to wait for them, a thin, stooping figure. Whoever he was he was known, and from the way the guard captain addressed him he seemed to be someone to be treated with honour. The sailor was sent off and the man led slowly up the steep steps.

Peering into the glare of the westering sun to see what was happening, Kenofer had not noticed Phormio running along the breakwater towards him, his wide, plain face alight with satisfaction.

"You saw? Do you know who that was?"

Kenofer smiled, suddenly glad to see him and already ashamed of himself; why was it always Phormio he hurt? But then he was always the nearest and it did not help that he never resented it.

"Who then? Only an almost shipwrecked man. But go on, tell me. You're going to anyway."

"The Master! You know, the bard from Phaestos in the Great Island you're always talking about. The one who hasn't even got a name because he's so famous!"

Kenofer felt something jerk inside him as if he had been struck. There was sweat on his forehead, drying cold in the wind. He said, not to Phormio but to himself and to the God whose hand was still over his hands, "The Master of the House of Singing Birds!"

He took one step back, his leg touched a stack of timber waiting to be carried up into the town, and he sat down suddenly. Phormio squatted down in front of him, trying to see what was the matter. Kenofer's face was pale and he had the inward-turned look of someone wondering if he is going to be sick. Then he looked up over Phormio's shoulder at the small bright figures that showed for a moment on the high guard platform under the pine-tree.

"I walked through that gate not an hour ago and I could see nothing ahead of me, no reason to put one foot before the other. Aglauros might just as well have shut me in one of his cells and forgotten where the door was. And now today, inside the same hour, he's here, the Master. I had thought with luck, with the greatest favour of the God, I might go to the Great Island in three or four years' time. And there, still with luck, I might have had the chance to hear him. And the God hasn't waited, he's here now. It makes me feel almost as sick as I did before Aglauros."

Phormio stood up, shivering in the freshening evening wind from the sea, and looked around almost as if the God of Kenofer were standing close behind him.

"Don't talk about Aglauros's prisons," he said. "It isn't lucky. And even if the Master is here, how can you hear him play? The summer festival isn't for nearly a month. He'll rest a night or two in the palace, play for the Governor, and then go south on the first safe boat. And you aren't allowed in the palace, ever again. Remember?"

Kenofer was standing too, looking up. "If I hadn't gone today, I might have found a way in after all. There's bound to be a party and I could have slipped in as a litter-bearer or a singer."

For a moment his dream seemed to have been put whole and shining into his hands, but now he could see that the high walls of Aglauros still stood between him and its fulfilment. Phormio, understanding as usual, put an arm round him and this time Kenofer did not shy away.

And yet! The lyre in its case hung from his shoulder, and the wind from the sea thrummed in its strings, like a soft insistent voice.

"Not tonight," said Kenofer, speaking aloud but to himself. "Tonight the Master will rest. It will be tomorrow."

He was studying the cliff below the guard platform, every detail clear in the level golden light of the sun, the rocks stained dark below by the waves that broke far up in winter, and higher by the drain that came out in a cleft below the guard-house.

Kenofer gripped his friend's arms, his eyes shining.

"No!" said Phormio, not needing to be told. "No, Kenofer. Those rocks are sheer, you'd fall to your death. And if you got inside what would you do?"

"Follow the God. It's his plan, he sent the Master. And who said I was going alone? You don't not want to come?" It was unthinkable.

Phormio, with a shiver of foreboding, knew Kenofer was right. It would not be possible to let Kenofer do this alone. And he knew with a sinking and certain heart that it would have to be tried. Only . . . who was this God of Kenofer's skill who could arrange storms and danger to the Master of the House of Singing Birds only for the good of his friend? Was Kenofer's skill as important as that? With the flesh and blood Kenofer talking as excitedly as any ordinary boy making plans for something he ought not to do it seemed impossible to believe. And yet the Master was there. It seemed that the God knew better.

2 ⚶ The Master Sings

The shaft of moonlight shining in through the unshuttered window of his room was still very bright. Kenofer stood uncertainly in the doorway, looking back. Everything looked small and tidy and very familiar—the water-jar and his best cup with the white stars which had come from the Great Island. The flowers painted round the window-frame by his father were red and blue in daylight but looked black now. The cover was thrown back from his bed and the lyre was standing forlornly on the stool beside it. It was far too precious to be taken on a dangerous climb, yet his shoulder felt strange without the familiar thong of its case.

Even if it was too soon to climb the cliff he could not bear to wait any longer in the house. He had told small Theano that he was going hunting very early, and his mother, glad that something could distract him from a gloom she was expecting to be overpowering, would not doubt her daughter. However, if she looked into the room she would not expect to see his hunting-boots and bow still in their usual places. He went back quietly and pushed them into the darkest corner under the bed. Now it really was time.

His bare feet were silent on the stone steps. There was no sound from the room where his mother and sister slept together, the only noise was the snoring of the old slave who slept in the porter's room beside the main door. Nothing would wake him before dawn.

The main door was stiff and would creak, and there was a quicker way out that he could climb with his eyes shut. From the bench in the courtyard to the sill of the cellar window, stretch for the beam end to the left and swing a knee up to the wall behind the house. It was a long time since he had done it in the dark, but he was still in practice.

Quietly as he had gone Theano had heard him, she had not been asleep. She sat up in the small bed in her mother's room and heard through the open window the stealthy sound of bare feet on stone, wondering where he was really going; from the way the moonlight was falling across the wall above her bed it was far too early for hunting. She did not expect Kenofer, so much older, to tell her things, but she was an observant child and she had been sure that there was more to his story of the Governor's unkindness than they yet knew. Now she was frightened again, as she had been so often since their father died; yet he had never filled her life as completely as her brother now did. He had often been away from home, working in the palaces of the Great Island. It had been eight years before she was born that he had come back from Egypt to find that he had a son and to name him for a friend at the court of Thebes from whom he had learned much.

Theano lay down again and watched the moon brightness move across the swallows her father had painted on the wall. Kenofer would come back safely, he must. When she had been speechless with grief for her father he had promised that he would always come, and she believed him.

Below in the street Kenofer went carefully among the mule-droppings and refuse that the stray dogs had not yet had time to scavenge. It was very dark between the houses. He took the quickest way, down steps that led directly to the harbour. There the moon still shone low over the cliffs above the roof of the palace. A torch burned in the gatehouse and a faint glow of light showed that other lamps burned in the courtyard beyond. In the town below all was blackness except for the wide silver path of the moonglow which spread across the still water inside the harbour wall. Even beyond the wind had dropped and the sea was quiet, whispering and nibbling at the rocks.

Kenofer stood a moment in the shadow of the last house, looking across at the breakwater. The shape of its black silhouette against the water changed. Phormio was already there.

His friend's bare shoulder was cold under his hand as they stood together staring up at the light in the gateway.

"I thought you might not come!"

Swinging his arms to warm himself, Phormio, who had been there an hour already and had hardly slept all night, said crossly, "Was that likely? Come on then, if we must."

He dropped down over the side of the breakwater and led the way across the black rocks, slippery and patched with barnacles. Kenofer trod on something sharp, slipped and swore, scraping his arm. They both stood very quiet then, listening, but there was no sound except for the slap of the small waves close below them.

"No, this way's no good, it's too dark. We'll be cut to pieces on the rocks," said Kenofer.

Phormio was inclined to agree with him, having thought so all along; a hope flared in him that Kenofer would see that it was impossible, but he had known his friend too long to believe it. They climbed back on to the breakwater; Kenofer, his arms tightly clasped round his cold chest, stood tense.

Phormio said, "While I was waiting for you yesterday, I was looking down the cliff. I was there a long time. If we had a rope there's a place where we could swing across to the ledge where the fig-tree grows just below the drain."

"And you've only just thought of it! Goat! Well, a rope shouldn't be too difficult to find."

There was one coiled up in the nearest boat pulled up on the beach. As they climbed the last few steps to the place where Phormio had waited, Kenofer was glad they were bare-foot. They could hear the night-guard very close above, he sounded restless and very wide awake. Heavy sandals shifted and there was the clink of a spear-point rattling against stone.

Phormio went first over the parapet; he had seen that part of the cliff in daylight, but now the moon was down behind the mountain above them it was very dark. His feet rustled in the scrubby bushes and a small stone fell down the cliff. Looking up, Kenofer made the snuffling whine of a dog who has missed the rat he is hunting. Then he felt a touch on his shoulder. Faint against the starlight the rope was hanging from the stump of a wild olive, but the ledge they must swing to was lost in the darkness.

His fingers were sticky with sweat and he felt cold. The dawn wind was stirring, beginning to move the grasses, then a gust sang through the branches of the pine not far above. It might make enough noise to cover them.

"Wait!" Phormio's lips were close to his ear and his eyes glittered in the dark. "The guard's changing."

There was the echo of heavy footfalls above under the hollow archway and the creaking of a door, Phormio did not wait for anything else; he kicked off into the darkness, swung back as his feet failed to grip and then pushed off with greater force. The noise of his landing was covered by a volcanic yawn from the guard above and a snort of laughter at what sounded like a barrack-room joke. The rope swayed softly back out of the darkness.

With an invocation to the power which had sent him out on this adventure, Kenofer launched himself into the dark.

Phormio's big hands caught and held him, pulled the loose end of the rope free and coiled it up round his body.

"Quick now, dawn won't be long!"

The drain was not closed at the top; it was like a deep groove in the rock. It led up and to the right, under the wall of the guard-house, to a difficult turn round a buttress of rock, and then they were out of sight of the torchlight, leaning back against the rough stone to get their breath.

"I wondered if any of the privies emptied into this, but they don't, it's just water from the roof," breathed Kenofer. "Look at that vine!"

It was as if the God's breath was on his shoulder again. Not far above, the vine which had looped across the arcade of the south terrace had sprawled down over the parapet. Without it the rock would have been too sheer even for a rabbit; with it to cling to there were toe-holds.

"I'm lighter," Kenofer whispered, edging past his friend. "Give me the rope." Now they had come this far it was his place to take the danger first. The young leaves tore under his hands and the vine creaked, but Kenofer was slimly built and could move like a mountain cat when he had to. It was three times his height to the parapet and by the time he had a hand to it the vine was shaking as if it was going to pull loose higher up.

Kenofer dropped silently on to the pavement below and listened. Inside the palace there were the first sounds of life; a dog barked and a well-rope creaked. Here on the south terrace it was still dark and quiet. He fastened the end of the rope and threw it down to Phormio.

It was all as he remembered from the day before, the couch where Aglauros had sat, the scaffolding where the painter had worked on the fresco. At one end a small pavilion, damaged in one of the recent small earthshakings, was being repaired; masons' tools and large jars holding water and plaster stood ready. Kenofer glided over to the doorway which led to the rest of the palace, but as he reached it, steps in the passage beyond sent him back into the shadow behind a pillar. Already the sky was much lighter.

A sleepy girl wandered out on to the terrace and across to the parapet. She emptied the jar she was carrying over the edge, set it down and stretched. A spray of vine-leaves, torn in Kenofer's climb, still lay on the edge. She picked it up and threw it down after the slops. A voice called not far away and she trailed back through the doorway.

Kenofer found Phormio beside him. "No, it's too dangerous. We'll have to find somewhere here to hide. Till tonight anyway."

Kenofer had been frozen with fear, now his mind cleared again. "Up on the scaffold, but drink first, we shan't have the chance later."

They scooped dust-scummed water from the mason's jar, drinking deep, and then climbed the scaffold. To the left the cracked roof of the little pergola was partly covered by the trailing vine. They climbed across to it and eased themselves down.

The wind which had risen before the dawn strengthened and blew a veil of cloud from the north-west to cover the sun, whipping up the sea beyond the two headlands into a pattern of sharp little white wave-crests. The hours dragged on towards midday. Now that the impossible had been achieved, Phormio slept deeply with his head on his arms, but Kenofer lay tense, aware of the flies, the gritty plaster on the roof under his body and his returning thirst. As soon as the light had been strong enough he had explored the roof far enough to make sure that they were not overlooked from any window higher up in the palace, and all morning the terrace itself had been deserted. As he had suspected the painter had only been put to work there the day before to create a fitting setting for Aglauros's cruelty.

Phormio, the practical, had a pouch of food fastened to his belt. Kenofer gazed at it hungrily, but if he touched it his friend would wake and Phormio looked exhausted. So there was time to realize what he had done and what harm it could bring to both of them, to remember Aglauros's eyes, and to wonder how he would punish Kenofer if he was found. Then, as weariness overcame him too, he twisted round close to the

comforting bulk of his friend and opened his mind to the ebb
and pulse of the tide of music that always seemed to be running
just below hearing in his mind. The words of a song began to
form, about the dawn climb and the courage of his friend.
It was as if the God's breath stirred very gently in his long
dark hair as it lay tangled with the vine-leaves on the dusty
roof.

Kenofer slept at last, and in his dream the sounds he had
been shaping changed from remembered notes to a different
rhythm in a different mode played on a lyre.

They both woke together to find the light striking the
terrace from the west and to hear music not far above. It was
a lyre being played in practice, repeating and refining, going
almost to the end of a phrase and then turning back. The
sound came from an open window not far away. Kenofer sat
up, his face awed and rapt in the look which had so often
excluded his friend.

"It's him, the Master. No one else on the island can play
as well as that. But what it is?"

As if the lyre-player had heard him the practice stopped
and he sang two verses straight through, but in words too soft
to hear. The sun, which had broken through the clouds, was
already below the western headland and the sea had caught its
evening glow. The lyre-player would be called soon to the
Governor's banquet.

Kenofer crawled carefully to the edge of the roof. None of
the tools had been moved, there were no cushions on the
couches, it was clear that no one except a slave to sweep had
been on the terrace all day. The music from the distant
window had stopped.

Phormio brought out bread and cheese and olives from his
pouch. They divided the food between them, eating slowly to
make it last and not talking much, both aware that the time of
greatest danger had come. The last light went from the sea
and lamps shone below in the town. At home Kenofer's

mother would be wondering soon if her son was coming home. There had been times when he had stayed out all night, hunting among the crags below the mountain peaks which crowned Kallisté, but she would worry all the same.

"Come, we shall hear nothing more here," said Kenofer.

They climbed back down the scaffold and drank deep from the water-jar. Then Phormio began to tidy his friend, straightening the crumpled kilt of old blue wool that in the dusk could have been taken for a palace servant's and refastening the clasp that held back his long hair.

"Wash your face, you've smudged it with your hands," he ordered. Kenofer bent over the water-jar, splashed himself cleaner and then dried his hands on his kilt.

"Now you."

"No, I'm not coming. You'll be safer without me. It's you who needs to hear. I'll wait with the rope ready."

"But . . ." Kenofer put out a hand and let it drop again; it was only sensible. With one there would be less risk.

Phormio put a dusty arm round him and pushed him towards the doorway. "Well, if you must go, go!"

It was dark in the passage which led from the terrace to the rest of the palace. The main rooms were on a higher level; sounds of laughter and the beat of a little drum came from the top of a flight of stairs. Kenofer ducked back into the doorway of a storeroom as a slave clattered down them and ran off into the dim light round a corner. The afternoon before he had hardly noticed the way as he had been led back to the main gate, but it was up those stairs, which led into an ante-room; the main dining-room was through a row of double doors opening into a little courtyard to the left.

Kenofer climbed the stairs. His memory had been right, lamps burned brightly in the courtyard and beyond the half-opened doors. Servants were passing to and fro from an archway. The kitchen must be that way. Someone was coming up the stairs behind him, Kenofer ran across to the half-open doors and pressed himself flat into the shadow made by the partly folded leaves and a large flower-pot.

Aglauros's voice spoke only a few paces away, gracious, slightly patronizing. The meal proceeded with agonizing slowness, then there was a flurry of servants clearing tables and the clink as wine-cups were filled again. Someone had been playing while the guests ate, but the Master was being kept till afterwards. Let it be now, soon, he was already so stiff he did not know how he would ever move again. For half an hour no one had passed, but if he was not back soon Phormio would follow him.

Aglauros spoke again, and then a quieter voice followed him.

"My lord, it will be a poor recompense for your hospitality." The leg of a stool grated across the floor, and Kenofer closed his eyes.

It was like walking at last fully awake in a beloved land one has known before only on the edge of a dream. The music was the song he had heard practised an hour before on the terrace, but whole now, with the words and the delicate web of sound that followed the last verse. Even beyond the olive-wood doors inside Aglauros's dining-room there was a hush after the Master had finished. Outside, Kenofer uncramped his clenched hands from the edge of the pot and tried to breath quietly, tears squeezing out from his still-closed eyes.

The Master played again, without words this time, a festival tune, solemn at first for the rites of kings and then breaking into the jigging beat of a country dance. Kenofer, quite absorbed, did not know that he was beating out the rhythm himself on the edge of the door and that the movement showed from inside the room.

It was Aglauros's restless eye which noticed the regular swaying and he gestured to the captain of his guard behind the Master's back as he still bent over his lyre. Kenofer, lost in the new world which he recognized as his own, did not hear the soft footsteps as the man circled round towards him from the far side of the courtyard.

Then hands fastened on his shoulders, lifting him out from his shadow. Kenofer arched his body, wriggling like an eel, kicking back at the unseen legs behind him. The man shifted his grip to an arm, twisting it across Kenofer's back. The sharp pain forced him down on to his knees, but still he wriggled, trying to bite. The guard struck him hard across the side of the head.

"Captain, your hunting was successful? Let us see what you caught."

The blaze of lamps dazzled Kenofer after the shadows outside, his eyes still streaming from the blow. He was kneeling on the floor by the Governor's couch, his arms still dragged back, looking at the wavy patterns painted on the plaster floor. There was laughter from the guests and a moving back of tables to get a better look.

"Show us his face." Aglauros had not moved on his couch. The sideways glance was one Kenofer remembered well, but as his head was pulled back for the Governor to see he twisted round far enough to glimpse the man beside him, grave, a little confused. His arm was instinctively cradling his lyre closer, while eyes like those of a kind hawk peered at the dishevelled boy at his feet.

"Master!" It was to him Kenofer tried to speak. Then Aglauros recognized him.

"The son of Megaros was forbidden to enter my palace again, ever. But he has come back!"

3 ❧ The Doom of Aglauras

The earth floor just inside the door was dry as far as Kenofer's hands could reach in the blackness, but further off the cell smelt like a midden and there was the sound of dripping water. He had landed on his hands and knees when the guard had thrown him in, and now he sat back on his heels, rubbing the bruised places. There was no light in the passage outside to come in round the heavy door and even though his eyes were getting used to it the cell still seemed quite dark. But it was night outside, there might be a window after all. He would be there long enough to find out.

He was not thinking about himself at all. Kenofer's mind seemed to have split two ways, one dancing off after the entrancing tune which the Master had been playing when he had been caught, wanting to play it himself, to feel it under his own hands. It was singing on in his mind like the quiet humming of a woman working at a loom. That and the song were what he had come for and he had heard them.

The rest of him was thinking about Phormio. Would he have heard the noise in the dining-room and had the sense to escape? It should have been quite easy over the wall with the rope, even if he had had to leave it hanging to show the way he had gone. They would not find him on the cliff in the dark. Or had he come up into the palace to follow Kenofer?

A shaft of light along the floor under the door answered him and there was a clatter outside in the passage. Kenofer scrambled back out of the way just in time as the door was thrown back and a dark shape swung between him and the flare of torchlight before falling across his legs, crying out in pain.

"Phormio! Steady, old goat!" His own body partly broke the other boy's fall.

At first they clung together, comforted only by each other's nearness. Then, as Phormio was still speechless, Kenofer felt about him carefully.

"Are you hurt? What did they do to you?" Then, as there was no reply, "Idiot, why did you have to let Aglauros catch us both?"

Phormio shivered and gasped. His voice came in a thin whisper. "There wasn't time. Suddenly the terrace was full of guards. Kenofer, is there . . . there is a window, isn't there?"

He was still holding his friend by the arms almost as hard as the guard had, and then Kenofer remembered. Phormio from a child had had a horror of enclosed places. It was hard to understand, but then his own fear of spiders was no more reasonable. Shutting Phormio in a cell like this was a far greater torment to him than physical pain would be.

"Steady," he said. "I think it's quite big but I haven't explored because of the smell. We aren't the first prisoners here. We'll see more in the morning. There must be a window because I can feel a draught."

They curled up together near the door. They were bare except for their kilts, and the night chill struck up at them through the stone of the walls and floor. Surprisingly Kenofer found that he was hungry, but there would be no food or water that night while Aglauros considered their punishment. It would be good to sleep, but he had dozed for much of the day and now all he could think of was his mother. When would she hear what had happened? He knew that she would go at once to the shrine of the Mistress for guidance.

But Kenofer followed the God who had come to him through

the power in his hands, bearing a gift that it seemed must be accepted at great cost. Each time half that he was given seemed to be snatched away. What blessing would be sent this time?

Phormio had slipped into a doze from which he woke with a start, suddenly even more frightened. It was a long while before Kenofer could quieten him. The hours dragged by in cold and discomfort and snatched sleep filled with dreaming. A little before dawn Kenofer woke for the last time with the other boy heavy across his legs, to feel the faint but unmistakable lurch of the earth moving. It was a sensation that no child of Kallisté could mistake, a gentle but certain stirring of some power that lay beneath the island. Outside in the passage a jar clattered as if it had been shaken over, but Phormio slept on and Kenofer was grateful for it. To feel trapped in the cell below the palace would have driven his friend quite frantic.

Light showed at last in a tiny window just below the ceiling. It was no more than enough to let them see each other's dirty faces, and the pile of rotting straw beneath it. Hard as the stones were they preferred to sit on them.

A little later a guard came with a jug of water and half a stale loaf of barley bread, but he had nothing to say and would answer no questions. The light changed beyond the window and it was nearly noon.

Phormio had not spoken for a long time, sitting hunched with his arms round his knees. Kenofer began to talk, not caring what it was about at first, nonsense from when they were children together, gossip from the town, anything to stir Phormio to life. In the end Kenofer too fell silent, but he could not sit still. It was five steps from side to side of the cell and he paced them like a caged panther.

The guards came at the second hour after noon, three men who led the boys out between them, up from the foul-smelling gloom and straight into the blazing light and heat of the courtyard outside the main room of the palace.

The night before Kenofer had seen only the flaring lamps

and the face of the Master when he was brought before Aglauros; now there was time enough to see more. They stood for a long while out in the full glare of the sun while in the shade of the pillared portico the Governor talked with his friends. The Master was not there. It was very hot, the shadows small and black round the bases of the great jars ranged along the wall, holding climbing roses and stiff clumps of white lilies. The tapering pillars were painted red and the guards' kilts were red as well; it was all red and white except for the blinding blue of the sky above. Two small almost naked children played with a ball and giggled at the boys, and a woman servant paused in a doorway, called to a friend and stood gossiping, looking them over. Kenofer felt Phormio still breathing as if he had been running, not yet free of the horror of the cell walls.

The tinkle of conversation from the group of shaded couches ceased and Aglauros crooked his two fingers again to the leader of the guards. The boys were brought forward to stand before him. The Governor studied them slowly.

Kenofer could feel the sweat running on his bare back, the waist of his kilt was sodden with it, and his hair hung loose and tangled round his face. His arms were held behind his back and he could not shake back the strand that kept falling into his eyes.

The Governor spoke to a friend, a large man in a robe of white wool, his head completely bald. "What would you do, Councillor, with a small pest which buzzes back again and again to plague you?" Two of the ladies with painted faces laughed.

The fat man swatted a fly that settled on his arm; his hand moved very quickly. "Like that! It would not come back again!"

"Yes, I begin to think you are right. Impudence leads to greater crimes if the hand falls too lightly. And now I have two flies instead of one. Kenofer, son of Megaros, at first you

35

only irritated me, now I think I am almost angry. As you failed to understand my clear words, you must learn from your own actions."

Kenofer was trying to stand quite still but it was difficult. He pressed his knees together to stop his legs shaking, and swallowed hard. Now, seeing Aglauros's narrow eyes, he began to understand what he had done to himself and to his friend. The Governor had no intention of letting him go with a beating, which would be fair after what was not really more than a boy's prank. It was going to be a quite different punishment.

"Captain." The guard stepped forward. "Take this boy to the south terrace; to the small pergola at the west end, the one with cracked walls. I have decided it is too damaged to be repaired. It is to be pulled down and the stone and brick thrown down into the ravine below, then we can build again. This boy is to do it, alone; you will set a guard to see that he is not disturbed."

"What tools may he have?" asked the guard, wooden-faced.

"Let me see. A pick, I think, and a basket. That should be enough to start with. It will be interesting to see how long it takes him. The friend who was unwise enough to follow him into the palace will be interested too, because he will wait in the cell below until the task is finished. How long will that be? Ten days? Twelve?"

"But Phormio . . ." Kenofer found that he was shouting, but a hard hand clamped down over his mouth and he was held firmly, wriggling and gasping. What this was going to mean to himself he could hardly take in yet, but Phormio was down on his knees between the painted pillars, crying. To shut him up again, and for days and days, and alone! Aglauros must know of his fear, the guards must have told him. Phormio would come out of that cell a shaking idiot.

There was not time to try to speak to him, even to catch his eye. Kenofer was led away, hearing behind him the polite laughter of the Governor's guests, and the shattered sobbing of his friend. He stumbled down the dark steps and along the passage, and out into the sunlight again and the wide view of sky and sea from the south terrace. While he stood, alone now, staring at the small part-ruined building, a guard was posted at the door and a pick and basket were brought. Then the captain gave him a small push in the centre of the back.

"Go on, you'd better get started. And don't try to get away over the parapet, we've already cut the vine back and you'd break your neck."

Kenofer walked to the edge and looked over. In daylight the drop was frightening; he turned, picked up the pick and went in through the cracked arch of the door.

Now that he was out of sight of the curious guard Kenofer found that he had tears in his own eyes, but they were tears of anger. Phormio had shoulders like an ox, but he must lie and suffer in a filthy cell while he himself, lightly built and with hands that must be kept supple and sensitive for the strings of his lyre, was set to do a man's work. And he must do it, hands or not, or Phormio would go mad.

Kenofer looked around him. There were two windows facing over the sea; a deep crack split the plaster above one of them, and ran part way across the ceiling. It seemed to be made only of plaster on matting over the beams. Kenofer remembered from the day before that it had not felt very strong.

He raised the pick and struck two or three inexperienced blows into the crack; one glanced off and nearly spiked his foot, but a small piece of plaster which he could lift with one hand flaked off and fell to the floor. He picked it up and threw it out of the window. The guard outside gave a sarcastic cheer as it rattled down the cliff.

After that he spent a little time clearing as much plaster as would come down easily off that wall. There were mud bricks below and a framework of wood. At least the building was not of solid stone; even Aglauros would not have set a boy to knock down that. If only he could make the weight of the building work for him.

He went out into the light again and climbed on to the roof. The guard took a step forward, saw there was no way of escape and settled back into the shade. Standing on a firm piece Kenofer began to work the pick along the crack in the roof. With luck, when that went, the whole corner would go with it. Plaster dust rose, clogging in the sweat that was running on his body, and his shoulders began to ache. The plaster came away only a handsbreadth at a time. Then his foot slipped and Kenofer fell hard, jagging his left hand across the sharp edges of the exposed matting. It bled at once; several large drops fell on to the dusty roof before he had time to wrap it in a fold of his kilt.

He climbed down awkwardly, one-handed, and washed it in the mason's water jar, drinking deeply first. The cut still oozed, deep across the ball of the thumb.

He began to try to pull the hem off his kilt, but the stuff, though old, would not tear. The guard lounged out into the sunlight and wandered across. He looked around to make sure that no one could see them.

"Here, let me have a look. Now hold still." With the point of his knife he cut a strip from the kilt and bandaged the hand. "It never works, tying knots with your teeth," he said to no one in particular. "Now, don't go at it all at once like a new bull with the dancers."

He was muttering something about a man's job when he went back to his place in the shade, and ungracious as he had been, Kenofer did not now feel quite so alone.

It was four hours before the sun dipped behind the hillside above the palace and it was too dark to work. By then Kenofer had already been sitting for some time against the warm wall, his throbbing hands resting across his knees. He ached all down his back from shoulders to ankles, his head was pounding and each small scratch and graze on his body had stiffened. He felt as if he had fallen over a cliff. Worst of all were his hands, the left swollen, too painful to touch, and the right sticky with oozing blisters.

Perhaps a quarter of the roof had fallen in, but that was all he had to show for the painful hours.

The captain came to relieve the guard. He hardly glanced across at the pergola. "Come on," he said to the boy, who had not moved. "Bedtime below!"

Kenofer followed him down the corridors that led to the cells. It was already quite dark there. He listened outside the door but no sound came from inside even when it swung open.

It closed and Kenofer stayed on his feet. "Phormio?" He could hear the apprehension in his own voice.

Something stirred and moaned close by his feet. He knelt down and felt for the other boy.

"I'm here, hush, I'm here."

Then his friend was clasping his knees, shivering as if he had marsh fever. Kenofer crouched down and put his arms round him. Phormio grasped him tightly and for a little they did not speak. It was no time to say "Why did we come?" or for Kenofer to ask his friend's forgiveness; they were both in pain and distress too deep for that. But who could have guessed the depths of Aglauros's cruelty?

Then Phormio felt the bandage on Kenofer's hand, and touching him carefully in the blackness found the other scrapes and bruises. For a long time Kenofer was too tired to eat. He lay with the other boy's arm across him, his head throbbing with the pain of long hours in the blazing sun. They both slept in the end, huddled for warmth as they had the night before, waking and dreaming.

It was in a dream that Kenofer felt the floor shift beneath him, a dream of the roof with the cracks widening and tilting towards the sickening drop from the terrace. Then he was awake as the stones of the floor seemed to rise and sag, jerking first away and then back, throwing the two boys apart. There was a noise of grinding and roaring, dust fell on their upturned faces and a splitting crash came from the far side of the cell. Outside the door a guard screamed and there was a distant roar like an avalanche of stone. Then quiet; the building seemed to settle and then stay still. Much further away there were still cries and frightened voices.

As the dust cleared Kenofer saw moonlight across the floor of the cell; the window seemed much larger than before. It was a little while before he understood that the stones below it had fallen and cracked outwards. Perhaps now there was a way to escape.

Then he saw Phormio lying motionless at his feet. He bent quickly to him, but the voice of the God below the island had not hurt his friend, he had only fainted in his fear. There could be no escape for Phormio. Kenofer splashed the last of the water from a now broken jug over his face and then sat with his friend's head in his lap, waiting for morning. He had been frightened at first, trapped below ground in the cell, but not now. They had not been killed, and surely it was not quite an accident that a God had spoken now, on this night when he had been so without hope.

Kenofer spread the stiff fingers of his hands across his knees and began to massage them gently.

4 ⚮ The Hand of a God

The guard came soon after dawn; when he saw the shattered wall of the cell he hustled Kenofer quickly up the steps to the courtyard. The boy felt Phormio's eyes on his back. hopeless and full of pain like a beast's awaiting sacrifice, as the door swung to between them. Phormio had not spoken a word since the earthshaking. What he suffered now was too deep for talking.

The main courtyard of the palace was in confusion. A large crack had opened in the wall above the painted arcade, and Aglauros, still in a bed-robe, was supervising the men who were already carrying in timber to shore it up. Women were carrying baskets full of broken pottery out of a small storeroom and one of the tall lily jars lay smashed across the pavement, shedding earth and dying flowers. Dust and rubble crunched underfoot.

No one had any attention to spare for Kenofer as he was taken down the stairs to the terrace to continue his task; he was surprised that the guard had remembered to come for him. His hands were still so swollen that he did not know what he would be able to do, but perhaps the God would show him.

The guard stopped dead in the doorway to the terrace with an oath, and Kenofer bumped into him. The man jerked round and took him by the arm; Kenofer could feel that he was trembling.

"By the Mistress, look at that!"

It was clear that no one had been down to the terrace that day since the earthshaking. Great cracks had opened across the paving and part of the parapet had fallen outwards, but at the west end where the pergola had stood the day before, there was nothing, only the sloping rock on which the terrace had been built. It was as if a great hand had come down and swept the walls away as a child wipes out a sand-castle.

The guard drew back from Kenofer, staring at him in wonder and fear, and then pushed him away. As the boy picked himself up he heard the guard's sandals clattering on the steps up to the courtyard.

He walked carefully across to the edge where the parapet had been, stepping over the cracks. Far down below, the waves were already eating into the pile of broken plaster and stone which lay at the foot of the cliff. The task which Aglauros had set him had been done; a hand stronger than his own had indeed come and taken the work from him. The feeling of relief was so strong that there had not been time for fear to follow it when the sound of excited voices came from the staircase. The captain of the guard was leading and after him came Aglauros, his face an ugly dark red. Behind them were the steward, one of the painted ladies, her hair hanging and a cloak caught up over her shift, and a handful of palace servants.

The sun was just over the eastern headland, striking the shattered corner of the terrace and gilding Kenofer's thin brown body as they found him standing there quietly, his back to the gaping hole, waiting for them. The Governor came part of the way across, only as far as the first of the cracks, but far enough to see what had been done. His mouth opened and then shut; for once he was speechless. The woman caught at his arm, but he shook her off so that she stumbled and began to cry.

Kenofer looked him straight between the eyes and this time his legs were not shaking. "It's done."

Aglauros turned to the captain. "Out! Both of them, at once. Get them out and see them clear down as far as the town."

"My lord, we should make offerings," quavered the steward.

"Later."

Kenofer walked back across the cracked floor, his head up. Once he paused to look at the partly obscured painting of the dolphins which his father had made with such skill. He would not see that again. He passed the Governor without a glance and went ahead of the captain up the stairs.

Then there was a pause while Phormio was brought, and he stood quietly, already feeling the beginnings of the chill of understanding that he knew would come and hoping to keep it back at least till they were clear of the palace. Word must already be spreading, because guards and servants were peering round columns and whispering in doorways. Then an older man with a face that he knew came out, followed by a servant carrying two panniers packed for a journey. It was the Master.

Kenofer took a step forward and then stopped. It was difficult to remember that he had endured so much to hear this man and yet that the Master could have known almost nothing of it, no more than an unexplained interruption to a dinner-party. He would not have heard yet, if he ever did, of what had happened on the south terrace. But for a moment their eyes met, the kind hawk's gaze saw the boy, who except for the dignity of the way in which he stood alone might have been an unkempt goatherd. He noticed the deep-set eyes fixed on him; then he was led away down the passage to the gatehouse and down to the harbour.

Phormio came out into the light, half carried by a guard, blinking in the sun, his face chalky-pale. When Kenofer went to him no one prevented him.

"Come, we can go. It's over, the God did it." Phormio did not understand, he had heard only one word. Panting for breath as if he had been suffocating down in the cell, he stumbled out into the middle of the courtyard and towards the gateway. Taking an arm from behind to steady him Kenofer followed.

The doors swung open and they were out again on the platform high above the town beneath the pine-tree. Already the warm clean smell of it in the sun was strong. Phormio breathed deeply of that and the fresh wind from the sea, and then they went down into the town. The guards followed a few paces behind, nervous and muttering together.

Kenofer was thinking fast. He must take Phormio home; the boy's family would never forgive him for what had happened or understand, but at least his friend was safe now and, with the favour of the Mistress, would begin to forget. His mother must make the offerings. Would she be home already or in the shrine at the end of the small valley above the town, where the mountain's southern spur split into high cliffs scored with caves and rock-falls?

They had come down as far as the first houses. It looked as if there had been little damage. In the night he had feared for his own home, but it seemed there was no more than the usual broken pottery and shed roof-tiles that followed any of the many small earthshakings that Kallisté had grown used to. Only in one place a half-built wall had fallen outwards across the street.

Phormio lived near the harbour. Just below his door the guards turned and left them, hurrying gratefully back up the hillside without a backward glance. The boys looked at each other, Kenofer searching his friend's face . . . if he still was his friend.

"They told you? What happened? I wish you'd seen it. It was as if . . ."

"As if your God had moved. Yes, they told me. Kenofer . . ."

With amazement Kenofer saw that what was behind his friend's eyes was no longer fear, or even resentment, but something like awe, awe of him.

44

Phormio picked up Kenofer's hands, swollen under the filthy makeshift bandages. "He knew and he didn't want them hurt. I understand now; we didn't go to the palace of ourselves, we couldn't help it."

While Kenofer was still speechless he looked down at the hands again, suddenly practical, and said with a shadow of his old easy smile, "Go on now, those need seeing to."

He gave Kenofer a little push and turned in under his own gateway. The boy stood looking after him, wondering if he had the strength himself to climb up the hill, but people were beginning to look at him strangely. Better to go home before the full story of what had happened was known. Head down, aching hands cradled against his body, he stumbled up the steps that led to the upper town.

It was late in the morning when he sat in the chair carved with birds' feet which had belonged to his father, in the upper room at home. He was looking sleepily at the familiar painting on the wall of swallows flying above a flowery hillside, and nursing his bandaged hands in his lap. Little Theano, who was neat-fingered, stood behind him to comb the last of the tangles out of his damp hair with great gentleness. Across on a couch, her feet tucked up under her billowing skirts, for she was still wearing her priestess's dress, sat his mother.

Comfortably wrapped in a thin old houserobe of hers, Kenofer felt very clean and only a little tired now. His mother and the housekeeper had spent a long time scrubbing him clean of the dirt and prison smell in her own pottery bathtub, and rubbing herb-scented oil into the bruised places. She already knew or had guessed much of what had happened, but before he could rest she must be told it all.

"The first night, after I got word from my friend in the palace, the embroideress, that you were there, I was wondering whom I knew with an arm strong enough to beat you as you needed to be beaten," said his mother thoughtfully. "The second night, when I had heard more, I knew this wasn't your doing alone. The Mistress has taught me to know the signs. It was a crazy thing to do. Was the need for it as strong as that?"

Kenofer felt tears prick behind his eyes, thinking of his mother alone through the long dark hours.

"Careful," he said to Theano, who had reached a knot. She gave his neck a small, loving pat. Kenofer looked down at his hands again, moving the fingers carefully within the bandages.

His mother followed his look. "If you do nothing at all with those hands for three days they'll heal clean. If you try to hurry they'll fester and it will take a month. And you can't wait a month—nor us with you! It's been quiet in the house."

She smiled then for the first time. She was small like her daughter, with beautiful eyes; her face was still painted and her hair coiled high as she had dressed it for the morning offering that she had made at the shrine of the Mistress. Kenofer realized that he had not yet answered her question.

"This year I've felt more and more as if I were beating at bars round me that I couldn't see. I knew there was so much, so much more waiting for my hands to learn than anything I had yet heard or found out for myself. It was as if there was some power always close behind me, as if someone was speaking inside my head, half telling me what I wanted to know, but when I tried it it came out wrong. It was as if I hadn't heard properly. People said I played well, I was the best in the island, better than the Governor's bard. But what help was that when I knew I should be playing even better?"

"I was proud of you," said his mother. "We all were. You remember your father, those last nights. It was only your playing that would quieten him. You gave him sleep."

Kenofer tried to push away the memory of the last days of his father's life; it was something he still could not manage, particularly when he was tired.

"Then I began to understand that it was as if something from outside me was trying to find a channel, trying to come through my hands. There were times when I played and more came from them than I knew of myself. It was then that I began to recognize the voice of the one who was speaking."

"Who was he?"

"Has He a name? I think He is the brother of the Mistress, the one who lives in the spirit of the wild things who run among the peaks of Kallisté. He speaks through the shaking of the island, but it's as if for me He has a gentler voice. I don't really understand."

In his mind he had a picture of someone young and dark and strong, His hand upon the sleek neck of a mountain cat. There was power in Him to make and do and create, a different power from the fruitfulness that His sister the Mistress gave to women. He had heard His laughter and there was something in it that made him afraid.

Now he was suddenly almost asleep and his mother noticed it. She rose and came to stand by his chair, her small hands stroking back the tendrils of hair which had already dried round Kenofer's high forehead.

"I will make a special offering. Perhaps the chief priestess will know what we should do. Come, it's time to sleep now. You're not hungry yet?"

He shook his head and then stood up and stretched; already he was stiffening after his bath. Glancing across at the window-sill he saw his mother's own small plaster table of offerings with flowers and barley cakes which had been put there freshly since he had come into the house that morning.

Theano came to stand beside him, and he put an arm round her thin shoulders and hugged her so that she felt safe enough to ask the question that was in her mind.

"Why does the Governor hate Father so much, even after he's dead?"

The priestess looked across at her two children. Theano

would barely understand, but would what had happened have been prevented if Kenofer had known before?

"It isn't easy to tell, it was so long ago and I tried to put it out of my mind. The summer I was promised to your father, but before we were married, I was already serving the Mistress. The Governor, Aglauros, had not long come to power; he had been waiting a long time for his father to die. I think he felt that now he could do anything. He saw me dance at the summer festival and he wanted me."

"He wanted to marry you?" asked Theano in horror.

"Something like that." The priestess saw that Kenofer had understood. "But I had already chosen your father and I would not go to him. I think it was only the protection of the shrine of the Mistress that saved me, for my own father would have sent me to the palace, there would have been no shame if I was willing. But I was not."

"Then was it dangerous for Father to have married you?" asked Kenofer.

"I suppose for some men it would have been. Megaros was not a man to be influenced so easily. But Aglauros has waited. I thought he had forgotten, for I have kept out of his sight when that was possible. Now I have no husband and after all these years he has found a way to hurt me."

"But a God saved Kenofer and punished the Governor, so it's all right now," said Theano happily. "I'm going to make a wreath of flowers to put on Mother's altar to show that I'm grateful."

She ran out into the sunny courtyard to pick flowers from the climbing vine.

"If it was as simple as that," said her mother, looking after her. "Oh Kenofer!" And yet if it was so simple the dread of it would be more than any of them could bear.

Then she saw that her son had hardly heard the end of what she had been telling them; he was standing more than half-asleep, fidgeting with the bandages that covered his throbbing

48

hands. She led the way while he trailed behind her, holding the robe round him, to his own small bedroom. The shutters had been closed against the sun, but it was still stuffy. His mother opened them—the sun was off that wall now—took the robe and covered him lightly with a sheet. Kenofer sighed, settled over on his side and seemed to sleep almost at once. His mother stood a moment longer looking down at him, at the strong bones of brow and jaw so like her husband's; then she closed the door quietly. Outside Theano was waiting for her; she took her mother's hand and they went back down the stairs together.

"He's come back to us, I thank the Mistress for that," said the priestess, and then wondered in her heart who it was that the Mistress had sent to her down from the prison of the Governor and the hand of a different God.

5   Above the Town

Kenofer set the lyre down, and fidgeted absentmindedly with one of the patches of dry skin which were still flaking off his hands. It had been ten days, the cuts had healed as his mother had foretold, and he could play again. The song that the Master had sung in the Governor's palace had been waiting, each note remembered, and he could play the melody, each intonation and phrase correct; it was only some of the words he had forgotten.

He was sitting on the hillside above the town, with warm rock behind him and the shade of an ancient olive to break the afternoon sun. It was the first time he had been so far since the day of the earthshaking; when he had left the house before, there had been strange looks in the street and he had known that people were talking about him. It was clear that something of what had happened in the Governor's palace was known, but not understood, and he did not yet see how he could speak about it to those who would not understand the gift and the burden of the God.

The day before he had suddenly felt strange again, sick and irritable and uncertain, as if he were still waiting for something frightening to happen, not recovering from it. Today the feeling was still there but he had succeeded better in hiding it from his mother, who had thought he was getting fever. Yet still the clatter from the narrow street outside and the tuneless singing of their servant had seemed to hurt him with an ache that was not really a headache. Up here it was quiet, the light filtered golden through leaves which rippled half-grey half-silver when the breeze caught them. But there was little wind; the air felt hot and still, thundery. Even the sea below was calm, lying like skeins of pale watered silk until it merged with the heat haze which hid the horizon.

Kenofer stood up and stretched; he had worked long enough for one day. The town lay below small and bright, almost like one of his sister's painted toys. The columns of the palace were dark red, and yellow nets were spread to dry across the beach. The scout-boat had gone, and the damaged galley from Melos, and there were only small fishing-boats pulled up in the harbour. Below the rocks where he sat he could hear a donkey's feet move along the track through the vineyards, but its body was hidden under a great mound of hay brought down from one of the higher valleys. Phormio had said that he would come back this way; his father had sent him on an errand to a farm across the island. He wanted to talk to Phormio. They had met since the day of the earthshaking but not yet talked properly, and Kenofer still felt alone and lost with the thing which had happened. Usually the skill in his hands could put things which troubled him into a pattern of music, but so far there was no pattern for what was in his heart.

The breeze stirred again in the silver branches and then dropped; the heat pressed more heavily and a few dried leaves floated down to lie in the furrows of the baked earth. Kenofer's head began to ache. Phormio was late and perhaps it would be as well not to wait for him; feeling as he did now they would only quarrel.

Suddenly the thought of the cliffs behind seemed to press heavily like a weight on his neck. He scrambled down from his perch, slinging the lyre over his shoulder, and started towards the path. At a place where it turned, dropping down from one vine terrace to the next, he stopped to look back. His friend might be close behind him after all.

It was then that he felt the beginning. A vibration, then a

sound like thunder in the ground coming from far beneath him. Then there was a hush, the sun was behind a cloud and the birds had stopped singing. Down in one of the orchards a dog howled.

Then the awful moving began. Kenofer was thrown to his knees; he tried to protect the lyre, but the thong broke and it slid away down the path. He got the crook of an arm round a tree that grew at the edge of the track and held on. The ground was now shaking like the bottom of a small boat caught in a storm and a crashing roar was growing all around him. Kenofer held on with both hands. A scatter of small stones fell around him and there was dust in his mouth. Clinging with all his strength to the creaking tree he looked up and saw the cliff beneath which he had been sitting such a short time before break off and fall outwards in a roaring mass of stone and uprooted trees, to crash down on the green vine terraces further to the left.

Then the stones which had been built into a wall to hold the road just above gave outwards and crumbled down almost on top of him, the path split into great cracks deep enough to have taken the donkey and its load of hay, and he felt the roots of the tree he clung to beginning to give. The trunk, and Kenofer with it, swung out in a great arc so that he fell on to the thistles and sharp shrubs that lay below.

All the time the roaring had not ceased. He lay with his head buried in his arms, not knowing where he was hurt. More rocks fell, but smaller ones, then there was only a patter of dust. It seemed that a long way off someone was screaming, on and on, on the same note.

It was difficult to tell how long it was before he was aware that the valley was quiet. Kenofer crawled backwards out of the bushes, pulled the long spines of the thistle out of his skin and looked around him. He was still alone on the hillside, with the sun's light a dull orange now through the pall of dust. It did not feel as if he was badly hurt.

Very carefully he climbed back to where the path had been, up the slope of stones and clay that were once the terrace wall. Then he began to search for his lyre. Although it seemed absurd that something so fragile should have survived the anger of the earthshaking he thought that he would find it and he was right; it was caught in the branches of a fig-tree, with two strings broken and one of its graceful arms half wrenched away. He knotted the carrying thong shorter, slung it over his shoulder and turned to look down over the town.

It was no longer there. From where the neat houses with their white plaster and bright colours had stood, a cloud of dust rose and oily smoke was already streaming up in several places. The town was as shattered as the passages of an ant's nest that an ox has trodden on. To the west the whole front of the palace had fallen into the sea and the inner rooms gaped open; flames were licking up from an oil magazine in the cellars.

Home! Kenofer could not see his own house from where he stood. He turned to run down the path, only the path was no longer there, only a twisted morass of crevasses and splintered rock. Sobbing under his breath he began to pick his way down through them.

That night after it was dark, fires were still burning in the town. Kenofer was huddled alone at the far end of the beach, in a cloak he had pulled down from the clothes-line in the deserted courtyard of a shattered house. Torches still moved among the ruins where people were trapped, but only the strongest men were any use now to dig for them. Further along towards where the breakwater had been the beach was piled high with the bundles and pots that people had been able to save from their homes. Women were weeping and there was the sharper crying of exhausted children. He had already been through all the pathetic groups looking for his sister, but she was not there, and in the dark and confusion there was no hope of finding her. He would search again at first light.

She had escaped from the ruin of their house, that much he was sure of. It had taken him nearly two hours to climb down through the fissured fields to the edge of the town. Their house stood high up and had escaped the fires which had blazed through the lower streets, but one side had fallen out, leaving the fresco of swallows that his father had painted open to the sky. He had climbed and called, but there had been nobody there. Then a weaker second shaking had come, driving other searchers screaming out into the open. Perhaps there had been time, perhaps a neighbour had come or the housekeeper had led the child to safety. In a corner of the courtyard Theano's singing birds drooped in their cage. He had climbed up to open it and let them go.

Then he had heard shouting and had forced his way down through the choked street to help the men who were digging out a family saved by the strong roof-beams of their cellar. By the time they reached them, Kenofer's hands were torn again and it was almost dark.

It was then that he had slowly begun to understand. The moment had come when there was nothing more he could do and thinking could no longer be delayed. In all Kallisté there were three people whom he really loved. Theano was perhaps alive, but he could not find her. Phormio would have been out on the road that edged the east slope of the mountain. Kenofer had seen one cliff fall and could only guess at the devastation further inland; it would be days before the smaller villages and farms could get help. He was trying to believe that his friend was safe somewhere out of the main path of the earthshaking, but he knew it was more likely that he lay under one of the falls of rock and broken trees.

His mind had shut away till last the thought of his mother. She too had not been in the town that day. It had been the time for the festival at a shrine some way along the coast and she had gone with other ladies, pretty in her flounced skirts with the tinkling gold ornaments and the elegant tight bodice.

She had kissed him before she went and looked at him approvingly, thinking that he was over the horrors of the Governor's palace at last. No news had come from the village to which she had gone. After Theano had been found he must search further afield.

Late in the night the flames that had almost destroyed the palace reached another oil magazine and flared up again, lighting the sky with a coral glow and shining across the water of the harbour in a pattern of crimson and gold. The flames made a path for fishing-boats from Melos, drawn by the light in the sky. Kenofer woke to the splashing and grating over the pebbles as two were beached not far from where he slept. Half-dazed with sleep he stood up, shivering, drawing the borrowed cloak around him, only to be knocked to one side as a group of terrified women ran crying past him into the shallow water.

In the confusion a child, clinging to his mother's skirts, fell and was not noticed. He lay screaming at Kenofer's feet. The boy bent to pick him up, but the child fought him, his face distorted with anger and fear. The women were swarming over the sides of the boats now, threatening to swamp them. The fishermen were shouting, even beating the women back with their fists. Kenofer carried the howling child down into the water; pebbles shifted under his feet and he almost fell. The child gripped his hair tightly.

Kenofer felt the rough side of the boat curve above him, a hand caught him under the armpit. He tried to disentangle the child and lift it up, but he found himself hauled up instead; the gunwale scraped him across the ribs, and the damaged lyre banged his shoulder. The child was lifted clear and he fell into the bottom of the boat, winded and sick. A girl caught hold of him and clung even tighter than the child had, crying "Nissos, Nissos," in his ear. Her tears were hot and wet, running down his neck, and she was almost strangling him.

He shifted enough to be able to get his breath, but her weight was still on top of him and he could not get up. Above them the sailors were silhouetted against the glare of the dying flames as they fought back the last of the women who were trying to climb into the boat.

Then he heard the pebbles grating again under the keel and the side of the boat lifted, they were floating, being pushed off and out of danger. Kenofer began to fight then, forcing his way up through the heaving mass of bodies as if he were drowning. The crying girl had loosed her grip, but a heavy man lost his footing in the swinging boat and fell across him, driving an elbow into his stomach. Kenofer bent double, lost to everything but waves of pain and nausea so that by the time he had managed to crawl to the gunwale to be sick into the blackness below, the town of Kallisté was already a coral glow far across the water.

"No!"

Still sick and giddy, he tried to climb over, to drop down into the oily swell. Surely it was not yet too far to swim? Theano was still there and he had promised that he would always come when she was frightened.

But hands pulled him back. "Poor lad, the sights he's seen have half crazed him." The sailor's voice had the rough accent of Melos. "Come on now, you have a sleep. No sense in killing yourself when the God has spared you."

"But my sister! She's there, I must get back."

"Poor child," said a woman's voice. "Like as not he's seen his whole family brought out dead from his home and can't take it in yet."

"Dead or alive, we're not going back; we'd lose the boat. There are hundreds still on the beach."

A small wave broke below and splashed his face. Kenofer crawled down into the fishy-smelling crowded dark. The girl who had clung to him was still crying. He patted her awkwardly, and then when she turned towards him put an arm round her. Part of him was numb again now that there was nothing else he could do but wait; it was difficult to remember that he was not the only one in pain.

When the girl stopped crying he asked "Who's Nissos?"

She gulped and hiccupped. "My husband. We married last month."

"Where is he?"

She did not answer but cried again.

Theano, curled between bundles of sailcloth in a shipwright's cellar close to the harbour, was far beyond crying. She did not remember how she had got there, she did not know where she was, only that she had seen the house wall falling and had run. Now that she had burrowed deep like a frightened animal she could not see the glow of the fires or hear the screaming of those who were still trapped. At first she had cried for Kenofer, but he had not come yet. But he would, he had promised. She was thirsty and her leg hurt where she had fallen on the steps above the harbour, but mostly the pain was inside her, growing bigger and bigger as the waiting went on and on.

Next day a galley bound south for the Great Island hove to and took most of the refugees from the fishing-boat on board. Few had wanted to go to Melos, the fishermen's home, and there had been only a small store of water. Kenofer went with the rest, there seemed no reason to go one way more than any other. The only direction he wanted was north and no one would take him there, and there was no news from Kalliste.

They beached at Amnissos on the third day, among the first to come south from the stricken island; there was a crowd to stare but few people ready to help. Kenofer had been watching the long skyline of the island for hours; he had never left Kalliste before or dreamed that an island could be so large as this one. On the beach at Amnissos he had kissed the young wife of Nissos and given her to her friends and then slipped away into the crowd. Here he knew he was in the land of the High King, and his palace, the House of the Double Axe at Knossos, was not far away. But he did not want to see sights, only to go north, though his mother and Theano must be dead by now, or rather it was easier to think that they were.

He wandered up through the small harbour town in the fading light. It was full of the sea, like Kalliste and yet unlike, set on a long flat shore and facing north. He paused in the doorway of a fisherman's shack and a kind woman, sensing tragedy behind his saltstained cloak and sunken eyes, gave him a grilled mullet hot off the spit and a hunk of bread. He crouched against a wall to eat them and then turned into the road south which led away from the harbour and in among the little hills back from the coast. It was midsummer and the nights were warm, and the last few days had hardened him.

Later that night he woke from his first sleep and lay under the stars listening to the small noises of the night. He did not know if his God had spoken to him since the earthshaking, when his voice had turned to thunder; he had not listened. Now for the first time he was quiet and away from people.

The air was cooler and he reached to tuck in his cloak more closely. His hand touched the leather bag which held the broken pieces of his lyre and the strings gave a feeble twang. He knew that this was the only thing left to him. Kalliste had gone, his family and his friend, even his lyre, but his hands were left, the hands that the God had already protected. And he was in the Great Island; far south, somewhere across the inland mountains that he had seen from the boat, lay Phaestos and the home of the Master of the House of Singing Birds. It seemed that as all other roads closed to him this one that he had only dreamed of lay open. Kenofer slept then.

The house lay at the end of a small lane which followed the

steep slopes of a long hill, facing south towards the sea. The ground was rutted and baked hard, and the boy walked very slowly between the plastered walls painted a blinding white, putting each foot down with care. They were wrapped in rags padded with leaves and the bandages were dark with dried blood. He was only just able to walk, his face baked by the sun of the high mountain passes and his lips cracked with fever. He had asked several people and he knew now that the house he was looking for was not far away.

Kenofer heard the music before he reached the doorway. The door stood open to a small room leading to a sheltered courtyard with a well and a stone bench under a pomegranate tree. A thin man already past middle age sat there with a lyre in his hands, talking to three who were much younger. There was an air of great peace in the courtyard, the strong sun tempered by the bright green leaves and star-shaped vermilion flowers, and only the quiet voices to be heard, and the twitter of small birds in the tree.

He stood some time in the doorway; the fever was mounting in him again and he had almost forgotten why he had come, only that it was to be here, and now he had arrived he was at a loss. Then the thin man looked up and saw him. He paused in what he had been saying and the pupils turned too; one half rose as if to send the intruder away but the Master stayed him with his hand.

"Come in," he said, making room on the bench. "Sit down."

Kenofer walked carefully across and sat down. He had always been lightly built, but now his ribs showed and his eyes were sunken with fever. He was dirty and tattered, but the hands that lay across his knees were still beautiful and the Master's eyes had gone first to them and to the broken lyre still hanging in its case. Then he knew where he had seen the boy before; something in his bearing as he had stood in the doorway had given him away.

The Master turned courteously to his eldest pupil, asking

him to play. While the young man did so he watched the exhausted boy more closely, seeing in him something so fragile and so tightly strained that his composure would be as easy to break as the thin shell of an egg. The pupil finished his song and stood waiting for the usual criticism, but the Master had hardly been listening. Picking up his own lyre he put it into Kenofer's hands, and the boy's arm curved to receive it instinctively, as a woman's does when she picks up a baby.

"Perhaps you will play for us, I think you have that skill," the Master said gently.

Kenofer looked across at him gravely and then bent his head. He played twice, first the Master's own song, heard once in what seemed like another life, but still held note-perfect to flow from Kenofer's hands. Then, something that it seemed had formed itself in his heart as he climbed the long road through the mountains and Kallisté dropped further and further behind. Before he had quite finished his fingers faltered and he bowed his head.

The Master rescued his lyre and then took the boy's hands in his own.

"The God has blessed you richly," he said, knowing as he spoke, with a certainty that pierced his heart, that the boy before him held the power to become one day a greater master than himself.

"Has he?" Kenofer looked up. "I haven't played since . . ." He looked at the broken lyre. "For half a month. Since Kallisté."

The pupils, beginning at last to understand, bent closer in shocked sympathy, and it was the nearest who caught Kenofer as he fainted, and helped to carry him into the house.

6 ❧ The House of Singing Birds

It was ten days before the fever left Kenofer and much longer than that before he could walk again. At first he lay half asleep, seeming to be floating clear of his uncomfortable body, and only aware that the house was full of music. Once when the fever was at its height he thought he must have been taken to be with his God, but then the face of the Master bending over him with eyes full of concern drew him back to the knowledge that only one thing was now asked of him, that he rest and grow strong.

Soon after the fever had finally gone he was carried down to lie in the courtyard under the pomegranate tree, to watch and listen to all that went on. Then a day came when he was propped up on cushions and the Master put into his hands his own lyre mended and re-strung. Kenofer blinked back tears as he felt the familiar weight and smoothness, and then he bent his head over it and played, picking out the music of the song which had come to him as he crossed the mountains. The words he had fixed in his mind while he lay upstairs.

All the other pupils in the house were older than he, for the Master did not teach beginners, but as he watched them, silent and grave-eyed himself, he was puzzled that they laughed and played jokes on each other, and did not always understand at once what it was that the Master asked of them. The music his God had put into his heart was too deep a thing to be approached with laughter, it had already cost him too dear.

During these days the Master watched his new pupil, who had come to them so strangely, but whose place in the House of Singing Birds had never been questioned from that first moment. Even the least perceptive pupil could see that the boy from Kalliste possessed a gift which was quite exceptional. It seemed that he never forgot anything that he heard played, his mind took in music as a sponge takes up water, and he learned almost as quickly the words of the long ballads that each bard must know to entertain the barons and kings who would be his patrons.

A little at a time the Master heard the full story of Kenofer's dealings with Aglauros.

"A pattern is in the weaving, one we cannot yet see fully," he said, one afternoon when they were sitting together. "If only I could have guessed who you were—or rather what you were—when you were dragged into the Governor's dining-room out of the night."

Kenofer gave his rare smile. "I don't think it would have altered anything. You couldn't have changed Aglauros."

"His family are allied by marriage to the royal house of Phaestos, did you know? The blood cannot have run true in him. His sister married a near cousin of the king, and their son, Prince Geryon, is a very different man."

"I think I heard his name at home," said Kenofer. "He commands the king's galleys, doesn't he?"

"Yes, and I was told at the palace yesterday that he has not forgotten his blood-tie with Kalliste. His boats arrived too late for you, but he took off most of the refugees who wanted to leave the island and he is providing for a good number on his own estate or wherever he can persuade the other members of the court to give them work."

Kenofer had gone white, and the Master wondered if he had tired him until he saw the hands clenched around the base of the lyre.

"Of course, your family. I was slow to remember that. As

soon as you can walk you shall go among them yourself to learn what there is to be learned. But for now I think the moment has come for more practice."

Kenofer kept his head bent and prepared to concentrate completely upon the Master's instructions. The times when they were alone together were of necessity short and he did not want to waste a moment. From the other pupils he could learn melody; what he needed now was the technique to play it, the phrasing, the intonation of a line, the confidence to let the melody sing for itself.

Then his feet healed and he could hobble about the house. It seemed that he had grown up during his illness. He had always been an attractive boy to look at; now there was something arresting in the thin face with its high forehead and deep-set eyes, the erect bearing and the beautiful hands. Word had spread through the small town that lay below the summit of the long Hill of the Kings at Phaestos that the Master had a new boy who promised to be something special. Kenofer knew nothing of this yet; he had hardly been aware of the palace as he limped past it in search of the House of Singing Birds, and he could not yet imagine the life of the court who made up the Master's main audience when he was not on one of his many journeys.

When there was a festival, or an embassy from one of the other kings who ruled in the Great Island, or when the king gave a banquet, the Master was sent for, and usually one of his pupils went with him to carry his lyre, stand behind his stool and learn the skill in gauging the moods of an audience that is part of the craft of the bard. It was unheard of that a boy should be taken so soon, but after a month the Master judged that Kenofer was ready. Kenofer accepted his decision thoughtfully, as he did every part of his training, and with none of the excitement that the other pupils had expected.

He had often seen the Master in his bard's robe of blue wool, deeply fringed and beautifully enbroidered with bands of white and gold, but he had not thought how he himself should be dressed. A new kilt had been given to him, and so far that had been enough. But on the morning of the feast he was to attend, he went into the small room he shared with two other pupils and saw that a crocus-coloured robe lay across the bed. He stood speechless, not even touching it, until Strymon, who had tried hardest of them all to break through his reserve, said, "For pity's sake try it on. We may have got it too short, but you're about my height."

"It's mine?"

"Of course it is!"

"But I haven't, I can't . . . ." Kenofer's hands were bare of rings and he wore no other ornaments. The only treasure he had brought from Kallisté had been a thin gold chain round his neck, and that had gone a few links at a time to pay for food as he crossed the island.

"You haven't got to pay for it before you wear it," said Strymon patiently. "The Master probably thinks of it as a gift, but when you're famous you can give him one back if you like. Now, please will you try it on in case it needs to be altered."

Kenofer bent down obediently and Strymon dropped the heavy folds over his head.

"Wait a minute, something's caught," he said.

As the older boy turned Kenofer towards the light and knelt down to adjust the hem, it came to him for the first time that the quiet days in the House of Singing Birds were over and he must face a new world outside that he knew nothing about. Kallisté seemed very small and far away; even Aglauros, though an enemy, he had known from childhood.

"Tonight it won't be like the Governor's palace at home," he said thoughtfully.

Strymon, pulling a thread loose with his teeth snorted. "Certainly not! Did you really go past the Hill of the Kings with your eyes shut?"

64

"Nearly. Your king, what's he like? Is he an old man?"

"Inarchos, no. The old king died not quite two years ago, but already it seems a long time. Now stand straight and let me see if that's right."

Kenofer turned round slowly. Strymon seemed satisfied, but now part of the hem needed to be restitched. He folded the robe over his arm to take back to the sewing woman, and then noticed that the usually silent Kenofer still seemed to want to talk. So he sat down on the end of a bed, for he was a cheerful and friendly boy.

"What did you mean, two years seems a long time?" asked Kenofer.

"You heard nothing of our problems back on Kallisté?"

"No, I wasn't even sure where Phaestos was, and all I knew about it was that the Master lived there."

"I think the Master will be remembered longer than King Inarchos. He was the younger son, you see. His brother died when his father was in his last illness. If it had been a simple death—like a hunting accident—the stories would never have started. But people didn't believe what they were told, that it was one of those sudden fevers, and they believed it even less when the king married his own brother's widow. She was priestess of the Mistress, and they said that she hoped to find Inarchos easier to manage than his brother."

"But has he been a bad king?" asked Kenofer.

"He's not killed or stolen land or burnt men's farms over their heads, but he's—weak, I suppose. He's a quick-tempered man with a strange sense of humour, but when there's a word really needs saying it's the queen who says it. The barons don't like that. Look, you'll see nothing of this tonight, only it's as well to know. The palace may look as pretty as a hillside on a summer's day, but there are as many snakes in the grass. You look tired, you should rest now. You'll be standing most of the evening. I'll bring this back when it's finished."

During the afternoon Strymon came back to help Kenofer

dress. When he brought him down later to the courtyard the Master was there; he looked at the boy, observing the way the long folds fell unbroken from neck to hem and the formal tresses into which Strymon had arranged the hair. Each detail was important when one played before kings.

"That looks well," he said at last. "How does it feel? You aren't used to the weight; could you play?"

"I think so," said Kenofer, smiling suddenly and breaking the tension that was growing in the courtyard. "But it's so hot, and I'm not used to being wrapped up like this."

"That will come," said the Master, dropping his hand lightly on his shoulder, and handing him his lyre. "Are you ready?"

That first time, as Strymon had predicted, he noticed very little of what was going on around him or how the palace looked. His place was to keep close to the Master, not to speak or be spoken to, but to listen and serve. They left the House of Singing Birds when the afternoon sun was still high and climbed the road to the palace. Kenofer, his feet tender after what had been his longest walk so far, hardly raised his eyes to the impressive portico which made Aglauros's palace look like a country farm. He was led in by a side way, to wait in one of the maze of rooms until the court began to assemble in the pillared state hall on the north side of the palace.

Kenofer climbed the wide stairs, lined with guards and palace servants, a pace behind the Master. Already the high room, brilliant with frescoes and even more alive with the moving flower-garden of the ladies' dresses, was as noisy as an aviary. Only the highest lords of the kingdom would dine on couches round the king's seat, the others were there to watch and attend the great ones. The Master kept himself a little apart. He answered the greeting of the chief steward gravely, walked to his place, a stool not far from the king's chair, and sat down, taking his lyre from Kenofer, who stood behind him. Bending his head to hear above the noise of chattering and laughter, he began to tune the strings.

Then the king and queen came in, young, tall and haughty. While the courses of food were carried by and served Kenofer stood, shifting inconspicuously from one foot to the other, feeling the robe heavy upon him and the sweat running down his back between his shoulder-blades. Not far away a group of young princes were laughing together. He wondered if one of them was the Geryon he had been told about, but he could ask the Master later.

The Master ate nothing, but drank from a silver cup which a page brought him from the king's own table, and then passed it back, still half full, for Kenofer to hold.

Now most of the food had been cleared away; attendants refilled the wine cups and passed baskets of fruit and sweetmeats, and the king turned towards the Master.

"When you came to us last you brought a new song, a song of the sea. We would be glad to hear it again, and any other that you may choose." He had a narrow face and eyes set close together.

The Master rose and bowed, then sat down again, wetted his lips from the cup that Kenofer bent to offer him, and began to play. Kenofer had heard him many times now, but the beauty always came to him freshly, and even more so tonight when for the first time he saw the power of the music gradually quell the restlessness of the great hall with the standing courtiers, and servants still going silently about their duties.

When he had finished there was the brief silence and then the small sigh and excited buzz that all artists hope for to show that their work has moved its hearers, before he sang again. Kenofer had not been aware that eyes were on him as well, but the court of Phaestos loved a romance and a mystery, and the unknown boy of legendary skill who had been saved from the earthshaking of Kallisté had made a good story. Particularly, one of the princes was eyeing him.

He was rather older than the others, thickset, brown-haired and with strong shoulders that reminded Kenofer of Phormio.

67

His face he had hardly seen, but there had been a quick impression of large features and a mouth that though big was mobile and expressive.

When the Master had finished his group of songs the king raised his cup and drank to him; then the queen bent forward, whispering. Inarchos spoke again.

"Our ears have feasted, gifted one. Your new song is among your finest, but have you brought us no other new thing tonight? Will not your boy play to us as well?"

From the way that the Master's shoulders stiffened Kenofer could tell that this was unexpected, perhaps a show of the strange humour that Strymon had spoken of. He knew that there had never been any question that he should play, on this his first appearance. Then the brown-haired prince turned towards him and smiled, and Kenofer sensed a genuine interest in his gaze that was reassuring.

"May we not have a song from Kallisté?" he asked, raising his cup and drinking to Kenofer.

The Master stood up and spoke low in his ear. "I had not expected this, but the king can make trouble if he is crossed. Are you prepared to play?"

There had been no time to feel nervous. As he sat down on the Master's stool Kenofer was aware that a vibration was going through his whole body like the tension on a tuned string. It was the breath of his God and he knew it. Of course he was ready; what else was his life about now that everything else had been taken from him but to let his hands bring forth the music that was in them? It was the song of Kallisté that he played, the song of the beautiful island with her proud mountain and fertile vines as she had once been, and then Kallisté as he had last seen her, riven and shattered and hidden in dust and flame. It was not a song of violent rhythms or harsh anger, but the cry of his own heart which came out in a melody and pattern of words of great simplicity.

Hardly aware of the audience, he did not notice that after

68

the first phrase the hall grew quite still, even the servants crowding in the doorways to listen or standing with wine-jugs poised. The face of the king had changed too when he saw that his malicious joke had turned against him; but the tall young prince had been caught and held from the first note, and by the end tears shone on his cheek.

As the last phrase died into stillness Kenofer bowed his own head, suddenly a boy unused to palaces and completely over-awed by what had happened. Then the chatter of praise and applause began and strangers were crowding to congratulate him, but he was aware of only one. The Master bent and spoke in his ear. "It is Prince Geryon."

So this was the man whose mother had come from Kallisté. He had thought when he first saw him that he had a look of the men of the island, and Kenofer noticed with emotion the tears on his cheek; that had never happened to him before—to do that. He felt the prince's eyes upon him, very direct in their gaze, as if for this hour the unknown young lyre-player was the most important person in the Great Island.

"Some God has blessed you; I thank him and you too," Geryon said quietly. "Will you not play again?"

"No," said the Master over his shoulder. "Once is enough for tonight. Kenofer has not long recovered from the pains of his escape from Kallisté."

"Yes, indeed. That is a story I hope to hear more of very soon. We shall meet again."

Kenofer smiled gravely up at the prince. He had spoken no word himself and the prince had given him no gift, except one that could not be measured in gold, the understanding that comes only from a friend.

7 ✿ Prince of Myrtissos

The next morning he slept late and the Master sent no one to wake him. It was nearly midday before he came down into the courtyard, but Strymon was waiting for him, wanting to hear everything after a dull morning spent learning ballads by heart. Kenofer told him what he could and Strymon was filled with awe. It was then that they heard an unexpected noise outside the gate of horses and laughter and chariot wheels.

Strymon ran to the doorway. "Who can that be? They'll never turn at the end, it's too narrow and this path leads nowhere!"

Kenofer got up and stood waiting, suddenly knowing what was going to happen. The noise grew louder and suddenly erupted into the quiet courtyard. It was Prince Geryon, still holding his chariot whip in one hand, a brilliant figure in a kilt of turquoise linen embroidered in gold, with jewels on his arms and round his neck, and high gilded boots. He saw Kenofer and smiled the smile the boy remembered from the night before.

Kenofer went towards him and bowed low.

"Good, you're here. Now we shall have to back the chariot all the way down to the road. My father always said I never thought before I did anything. Ah, my humble greetings to the Master of the House of Singing Birds."

This was to the Master, who had come into the courtyard.

"You honour our house, my lord. Can we give you some refreshment? We have good wine, although I know you say that musicians drink only clear air and spring water."

He was smiling and it was plain that he liked the young man very much.

"Master, we have disturbed your quiet house too much already. I only came to ask your permission to talk further with your new pupil." He looked around him as if sensing that there could be little privacy in the small courtyard where every word would be heard by others. "They will be running down the new bull-calves from the upper pasture at Myrtissos today. Perhaps Kenofer would find it interesting."

Kenofer heard himself saying, "My lord does me too much honour," and going forward as the Master smiled his assent. He had a glimpse of Strymon's astonished face as he passed out of the doorway with the prince's hand on his shoulder, and then he was caught up in a confusion of rearing horses, shouting grooms, and all the small boys and servants who lived in the houses behind the high walls of the narrow street, enjoying the excitement. The prince turned him with a hand and led him towards the main road down the hill to wait for the charioteer to extricate the chariot. He looked down at the boy waiting quietly and shyly beside him.

"You haven't been in Phaestos very long; have you been up in the foothills before?"

Kenofer raised his eyes to the dark tree-covered knees of the great mountain which bounded the plain on its northern side, beyond the broken ground that lay at the foot of the Hill of the Kings.

"Since I crossed the passes from Knossos, I've only left the Master's house once and that was yesterday."

The prince looked at him in amazement. "Then you've seen nothing!"

"The Master has neither a chariot nor a mule, and my feet were too sore to walk," said Kenofer, smiling for the first time, unaware how it lit up his grave face. He felt suddenly unreasonably at ease and comfortable with this large, unpredictable man.

The chariot was brought out to the main road. "I'll drive," said the prince, taking the reins from the charioteer.

Kenofer had never ridden in a chariot before and the prince was a skilful but fast driver. He was too occupied at first holding on to the high sides and learning to balance his weight on the floor of plaited leather to notice where they were going. The road twisted backwards and forwards sharply down the north side of the hill and then out into the plain. The prince did not talk, and gradually Kenofer found his balance and began to enjoy the swift rush of air that made his long hair flap like wings around his face and chilled the bare skin of his body. The prince glanced across at him once, saw his enjoyment, smiled and drove on.

It took them an hour to reach Myrtissos, the prince's manor house in the foothills of Ida, a large and comfortable place. It looked like a small palace from the front, with high balconies facing south and east, but more of a farm behind, with the stockyards and orchards climbing down the steep slopes. The prince stopped the chariot in a flurry of dust and startled chickens outside the main entrance. A groom ran to the horses' heads, and he threw him the reins, jumped down and strode through into the cool central courtyard. The sound of a woman singing and the chatter of children came from a passage to one side.

"You must be thirsty." The prince's steward was already coming into the courtyard with a wine-jug and cups. Geryon dropped his whip on the bench that ran round two sides and drained his first cup at a draught.

"Is it going well out there?" he asked. The sound of lowing cattle could be heard even inside the house.

"I think so, my lord," said the steward. "Asterion has been out since dawn; the mistress sent for him to come in from the heat at noon but I don't think he did."

"Hm," said Prince Geryon. "We'll see about that first." Then he turned to Kenofer with one of his quick penetrating looks. "And you, I think, are already tired after your late night, with your strength not fully returned. The dust and noise of a stockyard might not be the place for you after all. Another time; we'll find somewhere quieter for our talk today. But first I must see if my son is making a nuisance of himself, and send him in to my mother."

He led the way through to the back of the house, chattering as easily as if he had been a young uncle back at home, not a prince of Phaestos. Kenofer, remembering the haughtiness of Aglauros, followed him in silence.

In a small stockyard between old olive-groves a herd of cattle were jostling each other, heads down, eyes wild, lowing uneasily. The fully grown beasts were wide-horned, their rough coats black or russet. The high fence around seemed hung with all the workers of the manor, and small boys climbed between them shouting. The stockmen were trying to cut out the half-grown calves from the herd.

"Asterion!" The prince's voice carried even above the pandemonium.

A boy of about twelve, thin and very dark, and as dirty as anyone there, turned his head, jumped down from the stockade and ran across to them.

"Oh good, you're back." The formal bow did not go with bare dusty feet and a kilt which, having caught on the fence, had a jagged tear.

"Yes, I'm back." The prince gave his son a quick hug and then held him at arms' length in exasperation. "Your grandmother was asking for you, I'm told. Will you go at once, please, and find out what she wanted, and tell her I'm here. And while you're about it change that kilt before it's past mending."

"What happened on the Hill of the Kings?" asked the boy, clearly in no hurry. "Who did you talk to?"

"A famous bard, a new one. That is, after only one day his fame has spread all through Phaestos, so I expect by the end of the month word of him will be all across the island."

"What's his name?"

"Kenofer. It would be polite to greet him."

Kenofer, trying to hide both amazement and amusement, bowed gravely; the boy, not the son of a prince for nothing, greeted him with equal solemnity. Then his dirty face broke into a wide grin very like his father's.

"Are you really a famous bard? Then why has Father only just met you? He knows everyone in the island who can play or sing."

"He didn't meet me because I've only just come. I used to live in Kallisté," said Kenofer, smiling back at Asterion's directness.

"Kalisté? But that's where . . ."

"Enough." His father stopped him quickly. "You had a message to carry, don't you remember?"

As the boy ran off Prince Geryon put a hand on Kenofer's shoulder and led him up a path away from the dust and shouting to the hillside behind the house. In a shaded place there was a view of the sea and a stone seat had been built. The prince drew down Kenofer to sit beside him and for a while they rested in silence. The stone was warm, the hillside seemed to shimmer with the heat and the steady pulse of the cicadas, and far away the sea was a dazzling bar of blue and silver. Kenofer felt peaceful and comfortably tired, the way he had felt last year coming back with Phormio from an evening visit to his uncle's farm.

Then the peace had gone and the pain was back worse than before for having been forgotten for a little: Kalisté and his mother and Theano and, worst at this minute, Phormio. In one month he had come from being the outcast of a provincial governor's hall to the companion of princes, but there would never be another first and closest friend, no other Phormio, whatever friends his future life might bring to him. Had his first small achievement been bought at such a cost?

The prince guessed a little of what he was thinking from

his face. He began to talk, not particularly to Kenofer, but looking out over the roofs of the house below.

"When I was a child I had a grandmother I was very fond of. One night, just before bedtime she sent me a toy that she knew I had been hankering for; I can hardly remember what it was, a model cart, I think, with a wooden donkey with legs that moved. She had ordered it to be made specially, and had it sent to me as soon as it arrived. I did not understand that she had been ill many months and had learned not to waste what time there was. Of course I played with it at once and cried when my nurse carried me off to bed. There was no time to thank my grandmother."

He looked down at the last tufts of summer daisies growing round the seat, but as if he hardly saw them. "She died that night, and since then I have learned that if someone has given me pleasure I must thank them at once; like my grandmother I try not to waste what time I have. In your song you brought me a special gift, both in the song itself and in the memory it gave me of Kallisté, which I loved from the moment I saw it but have visited only twice. Such debts are not easily paid, but it may be that I can be of some service to you."

"Last night when you thanked me," said Kenofer quietly, "you blessed the God from whom the music came. Others spoke of my skill, but you saw more deeply and that alone is thanks enough." It sounded almost ungracious, but as he looked across at the prince it seemed that Geryon understood.

"It has seemed to me lately that what has been given to me has been a very heavy gift to bear, and one that has already cost me almost everything I valued. What you said lightened the burden. It isn't easy to explain." He spread his hands in despair and fell silent.

Then, leading him gently across the difficult ground of his memories, the prince drew out the whole story of what had happened since Kenofer had first gone to Aglauros's palace.

When the boy had finished he sat a little longer and then gave him the grin that with his large mouth seemed to split his face in two.

"Yes, I understand something of the weight of your burden now. But you will have heard that I have refugees from Kallisté in my own house. Shall we go down to speak with them?"

Kenofer looked at the great house partly seen through the trees, and felt his mouth go dry and his heart begin to pound. He was suddenly sure that Geryon had news for him and had been waiting only for the right moment to tell him. Had he not silenced young Asterion when he had been about to speak?

The prince stood up. "Come, if there is anything to know it would be better to hear it quickly."

He led the way down the path and in through the back entrance of Myrtissos. In the courtyard a man on his hands and knees was carefully repairing the cracked plaster base of a pillar. He stood up quickly when the prince spoke to him, wiping his hands on the seat of his kilt; Kenofer recognized him as a craftsman who had often worked with his father in Kallisté. The man glanced across, knew Kenofer at once and spoke urgently to Geryon.

"Come," said the prince.

Kenofer followed him down a narrow passage which clearly led to the women's part of the house. The chatter of young voices came from beyond a doorway where light filtered down through a ceiling of vine-leaves. A group of girls was kneeling on the floor to sort out a great pile of newly washed wool into fleeces. Kenofer took a step forward, searching among the faces turned towards him. The chattering had stopped. Two he knew, a friend of his mother's and a girl seen once at a festival; and then there was a third, very small, with her back to him, who had not seen him come in. Someone nudged her and she turned slowly, to show a small face and enormous dark eyes.

Kenofer stumbled forwards into the confusion of wool and billowing skirts as the others scrambled out of the way, to scoop the small girl into his arms and hold her with a grip which squeezed her breathless.

"Theano!"

She sagged in his arms and he held her away from him, frightened that he had hurt her; but she had not fainted. It was only that everything had happened too quickly.

"Take her out into the air."

His mother's friend bent over the child. Kenofer picked his sister up in his arms and carried her down the steps and into a part of the garden cool in the shadow of the house. He felt Theano's thin arms come fiercely around him and her face burrow deeply into the hollow of his shoulder. He sat down with the child in his lap, held closely against him, and the woman who had come down the steps behind them brought water for Theano to drink and bathed her face.

"We found her wandering alone on the beach that first morning and brought her with us when the prince's ships came," she said. "All this time since the island she has hardly spoken. We could not make out what had happened to her and how she was separated from the housekeeper, and she could not tell us. We thought the pain of it had driven her wits away for good. Then we heard more news from those who had left after us."

Theano, her face still against his shoulder, shivered in Kenofer's arms. He looked up into the woman's kind, tired eyes and saw that there was more to hear.

"Tell me, I'd rather know. I've dreamed it all already twenty times," he said, feeling the tears already wet on his cheeks.

"You know that your mother was at the eastern shrine? It seems that the dancing there was over and they had gone into the priestess's house to rest. The walls were stone and they fell in the first shaking, there were only two who came out alive. They had mostly been asleep and were too dazed to escape. I think your mother died almost in her sleep, and quickly."

Kenofer put his face down in his sister's dark soft hair which was so like their mother's had been, and the woman went quietly away.

After a while Theano wriggled and he loosed her. She sat back and looked at him properly for the first time.

"You did come, but you took so long!"

He might have been an hour late for her birthday party. "Of course I came, I said I would. Isn't this a lovely place where you've been waiting for me? Do you like it here?"

She nodded, silent again. He saw that the shock had sent her back into her early childhood and it would be a while yet before she recovered. "Listen, I'll tell you a story."

He made what had happened to him into the sort of tale with which he had lulled her to sleep when she was small; before he had quite finished the prince came down the steps and stood smiling down at him.

"The Master will think I've stolen you. It's time I drove you back to the House of Singing Birds. No, little one, he will come again soon." This was to Theano, whose arms had tightened again round her brother.

"She has a home here with my mother for as long as you leave her with us," said Geryon. "That I can do for you, and for the child herself."

Then Theano, still holding Kenofer's hand, allowed herself to be led back to the vine terrace and handed into the keeping of her new friends. The prince's chariot was waiting for them outside the house; out of sight of the compassionate but curious gaze of the women Kenofer turned to speak to Geryon.

"My lord." He was only slowly understanding that he was no longer alone in the world and on the Great Island; he had a sister and a new friend, the first he had gained as a man, for he felt that his own youth was now long over. "I think there is only one way that I can repay you and that is with these."

He looked down at his hands.

"That will do very nicely. To play midwife to a new song, or a whole line of new songs, will be a noble patronage. And I may whisk you away from the Master from time to time to play for me and my friends alone?"

"My lord has only to ask."

Not too often, the prince thought, looking down at him. What Kenofer needed now was time and quiet. Time to learn all the Master could teach him, and grow strong again after his ordeal. But it would be a pleasure to show him the plain and mountains of Phaestos, he could already tell that the boy was not only a great artist in the making but a delightful companion, and Prince Geryon had never been one not to recognize a thing for its true worth because he found it in an unlikely place.

He stopped the chariot at a place where the road turned back on itself and there was a view of the foothills, the deep clefts between them dark with shadow as the level rays of the afternoon sun shone warmly on the upper slopes.

Sensing that this was a favourite view, Kenofer shook himself free from his own deep thoughts.

"That is Ida, but the country people call her the White Mountain, because the snow lies so late on her peaks. I was about your age when I first came to know her well," said the prince. "It was at the time of the Choosing."

Kenofer looked puzzled.

"It is not a custom on Kallisté? In the spring the boys who were born in the same year go up together to the mountain, and there they learn . . . many things. But mainly they draw a little closer to the mystery that dwells in the mountains, the young god who was nourished there. When they come down there has been a choosing among them, and those few are brought to the king and serve him in the palace for that year. It is the beginning of their manhood."

"There must be a song for the newly chosen," said Kenofer, his thoughts already throbbing with how it should be.

"There is a song for the priestesses but not one for the Summer Guard themselves. Perhaps you will make it for us."

He spoke to the horses and drove on. It was dusk when the chariot stopped in the road above the lane which led to the Master's house, and they walked along it together towards the gateway. The Master was waiting for them under the pomegranate tree and from their faces he learned much that it would not have occurred to Kenofer to tell him. The boy excused himself quietly and went into the house, suddenly almost too weary to stand upright, and the prince sat down on the seat beside the older man and told him whom Kenofer had found at Myrtissos.

"If I could have asked one more gift for one who is already burdened with them," said the Master, "it would have been for your friendship. I could not have foreseen what would happen last night, but I was already beginning to fear for the boy. Sometimes the wine is too strong for the wineskin. Without help he could still have broken, and the palace of Phaestos is not a safe place for someone like Kenofer to grow up in."

"I had wondered if I could take him into my household," said the prince. "But I saw almost at once that though I should enjoy it and probably he as well, it would not have been right. It would have been an offer hard to refuse, but when he is older he will need to be free."

"I was hoping not to have to explain that," said the Master with a glance from his kind hawk's eyes. "Kenofer has already travelled a hard road. He will sing at Phaestos and then in the halls of many kings even beyond the Great Island, as I have. There may be times when you can smooth his way in the halls of kings and times when you will enjoy simple things together. I think it will be an equal friendship for as long as your lives run the same way."

"May his God hear your words," said Prince Geryon.

8 🙖 Aethra

Theano heard the voices calling her name through the orchard, but she did not move, even though the prickles of a thistle were scratching her bare legs as she crouched under the low-spreading branches of the fig-tree. It had come again while she had been in the women's hall, a small earthshaking, and she could not bear it yet. Not here at Myrtissos where after three months she was beginning to open her eyes at last to look around her and enjoy what she saw, like a plant that is moved from a dark place into the sun.

She had run out into the garden as she had run that last time, and now again her eyes were shut and her hands were over them, and all she wanted was Kenofer. But although he came to see her when he could, and she was beginning to be sure of him again, and that he would indeed always come when she really needed him, today there had been a shaking and it was not one of the days when he was here. In her mind now, coming back over and over again, was a picture of the pretty cup that the lady of Myrtissos had just put down on the table beside her chair suddenly beginning to tremble, falling over and smashing on the floor, and the lurch of the floor itself as it moved.

"Oh Theano, do come out! It's over, and nothing's broken, nothing much." It was Aethra, one year older and the prince's niece, small, cheerful and black-eyed.

It was hard to say no to Aethra; Theano crawled out from under the branches and dusted the dead leaves off her skirt.

"Poor thing, was it like that at home?" Aethra was not ashamed of being curious.

Suddenly Theano found that some things hurt less after you had said them out loud; she had never realized that before. "It started like that, only it got worse and worse and didn't stop, so I ran away and the whole front of our house fell down in the road behind me."

"Where did you run to?"

"I don't know, nowhere looked the same any more. It was like a dream when you run and stay in the same place; I was running and the road and the steps down to the harbour were moving up and down too."

"Well it's over now, and we don't have earthshakings here very often. Anyway, it's dinner-time. Come on."

She took the younger girl's hand and began to lead her back to the house. But as Theano reached the foot of the steps she stopped and pulled back again. The lady of Myrtissos, tall and thin with the same kind eyes as her son, saw them and noticed the protective arm that Aethra had put round the younger girl's shoulders.

"Good, you've found her, and I see that you two are now friends. Aethra, I think it will do you no harm to have to think about someone other than yourself for a while. Perhaps tonight we should move Theano's bed from the big room in with you; that way you will be company for each other." She smiled benignly and moved away.

The two small girls looked at each other in amazement, then Aethra giggled. "This will be fun, but I'll have to move all my things. Come on." She picked up her full skirts and ran down the passage towards the stairs which led to the women's rooms and Theano ran after her, suddenly excited and distracted from her fear by the thought of a new room and a new friend.

That night, when the dreams that came so often woke her again crying for her mother and for Kenofer, almost at once she felt Aethra's warm fat arms hugging her and leading her across to the other small bed to be comforted. Then they whispered to each other in the dark till they both fell rather uncomfortably asleep.

The next day was a good day, because Kenofer came. The girls often climbed the hill behind the big house when they could escape from the women's rooms and the many skills that a young lady of Phaestos had to learn. Up under the old olives by the stone seat they could watch the road in comfort and see if anyone was coming from the town or the harbour, and the boys playing in the stockyards below. From the hillside that morning Theano saw the dust of chariots rising in a plume across the olive-groves which filled most of the valley between Myrtissos and the higher ground that hid the Hill of the Kings.

She stood up and shaded her eyes with her hand.

"Oh, is someone coming?" Aethra never stayed still long enough to look properly.

"Two chariots, no, three. The prince and my brother and other people I don't know."

They started to climb back down the hill. "Why doesn't Prince Geryon live here always if it's his home?" asked Theano.

"But he's here much more often than he used to be. When he was the king's admiral all the time he hardly ever came, he used to be away sailing between the islands. But he doesn't go so often now. His wife died three years ago and he wants to be with Asterion and I think he has had disagreements with the king. My uncle always knows what he wants to do at once, and how he should do it, and the king isn't like that. He asks the queen and the council and still can't decide. My uncle was very cross that more help wasn't sent to Kallisté by Phaestos and the High King at Knossos. Asterion said he took some of the scout-boats without permission and the king was angry, and that's why he doesn't often go to the palace now."

Theano was impressed; it put her rescue and that of the others from Kallisté in a new light.

"But won't the king harm Prince Geryon? Wasn't Asterion worried?"

"Nothing bothers him, he thought it was funny. I don't think my uncle actually disobeyed a royal command, it was just that he understood the king wouldn't decide in time for our help to be any use, so he went anyway. You know, like not asking to stay up late till you have!"

Theano giggled. For a moment it had frightened her to think that the prince, on whom her well-being now depended, might be in danger, but if Asterion was not worried then they were safe. She was rather in awe of him, as one of the eldest children and the only son of the prince. Then they heard horses' hooves outside and ran to hide behind the tall red pillars as the prince and his friends came into the courtyard.

Kenofer knew by now where to look for her. Today for the first time she ran laughing into his arms. This was something new; she had recovered fast after that first visit, but still had been very different from the child he remembered. He allowed himself to be led through to the women's rooms while she jigged about and talked excitedly by his side and he smiled down at the new friend, Aethra, who seemed able to work miracles overnight.

At noon he walked back into the men's hall, where the prince was talking with his friends. Kenofer paused, suddenly shy, between the folding doors that led from the main courtyard, he was still not used to the prince's informal ways and conscious of how much the youngest he was there. The prince had driven to the palace the night before to see if his friend Isander, the architect, a native of Kalliste although he had left it many years before, would come to examine cracks that had opened in the west wall of the house. The earthshaking that had broken Kalliste had been felt even as far as Phaestos. Now, after the second small quake, more plaster had fallen. He had sent word the night before to the House of Singing Birds that he was driving back, and Kenofer had been at the palace early.

84

The prince, Isander, and the others who had driven out with them, barons from the other side of the valley, had inspected the wall and now they were sitting in the welcome cool of the men's court while servants laid a light meal on small tables by their couches.

The prince saw him and beckoned. "Come in. The little one seemed happy today."

"Yes, she has a new friend, your niece Aethra, and she could talk of nothing else." He had been going to say something more but stopped suddenly, feeling a prickling behind his eyes. It had been so good to hear her laugh again.

Geryon, understanding, signed to a servant, who brought a small lyre and gave it to Kenofer.

"Play to us, before we eat."

It was an instrument that Kenofer had used before when he had been at Myrtissos, but it still felt unfamiliar after his own. He took it into his arms and bent his head over it, finding his way across the strings, suddenly lost to the room where he was and the watching men. Music came quickly and he moved for a while from one theme to another, not singing yet. Then there was a small jigging rhythm, Theano laughing with her friend. He played it till he was sure it would come again and then looked up smiling.

"I must find words for that."

"It comes just so, like water welling up out of a spring?" asked Isander, a thickset, grave-faced man, older than the others there.

Suddenly Kenofer was shy again, tongue-tied among these strangers now that his hands were quiet.

"No, tell us," said the prince. "You have a skill; Isander here has also been blessed by a God. You can learn from each other, although he speaks through stone and you through music. You were playing for Theano, your little sister?"

"You knew?"

"Of course. But so far all the music I have heard you

make has been for Kallisté. Have you no song for Phaestos?"

Asterion had come in and was standing behind his father's chair. "Will you make me a song for my year of the Choosing?" he asked, bright-eyed and eager.

"When will that be?"

"In five years' time."

"Five years?" Kenofer smiled and played a little phrase that sounded like someone slowly plodding up a long road.

"Quite!" said the prince. "Kenofer will not be needing to think of your song for a while yet. It's too soon for Phaestos, isn't it? Your music comes from a very deep spring, I've known that ever since I first heard you play. There will be time over the years to come to know us better, and then a song for Phaestos will come. It is not, perhaps, quite the happy place it may seem on the surface; we have a king who does not always see clearly and a queen whose sight is too sure, so I am not so often at Phaestos as I once was. But all of us here are loyal to the royal house, who have guided us and stood for us before the gods for so long, as Phaestos is also loyal to Knossos. When the time comes I shall send my son to serve the king in his Summer Guard, if he should be among the Chosen."

Asterion was quivering with impatience by his father's side. "Kenofer, will you come, I want to show you something?"

Kenofer stood up. He had not seen Geryon in this serious mood before and it made him uneasy in a way hard to explain. He was glad of an excuse to go out of the men's hall and into the sun.

"What is it?" he asked, as Asterion led the way out to the stockyard and up the hillside by a new path, to the west of the house.

"Not far now," said Asterion over his shoulder. It was clear that the place to which they were going was important to him and Kenofer felt honoured that he wanted to share it.

They came out on to a bare slope of the hillside crowned by

a stony outcrop of rock, high above the roofs of the house. It was very hot, the sun beating down from directly overhead, and Kenofer put up a hand to shade his eyes. They had been troubling him ever since the dustclouds of Kalliste and the strong light was almost more than he could bear.

Asterion turned triumphantly. "Now look up there, what can you see?"

Towering behind them the great foothills of Ida were cleft by a pass leading up through pineclad slopes to the skirts of the great mountain herself. Far up her dark crags were scored by rock-falls and deep gullies, but here, so close, her crown was hidden from them.

"I can see the mountain, what else?" Kenofer asked.

"Look, high up to the right, can you see a pine that's been split by lightning? Good, now even higher, a dark spot?"

Screwing up his eyes Kenofer followed the pointing arm. "Yes, I see."

"That's the cave of the Mistress, the place where the boys first meet together when they go up for the Choosing. The place I shall go to, like Father did, and Grandfather."

"I see. Come down out of the glare and tell me what will happen then."

There was only five years between them in age, but already, seeing Asterion's enthusiasm, Kenofer felt tired by more than the bright light and the steep climb. He liked the boy so much, but Asterion was so sure; it was not long since Kenofer had been sure in the same way, but following his own fate had already led him by hard paths and he could be certain there were more ahead. Asterion had a confidence that it seemed nothing could shake, neither awe of the gods nor any doubt that the weak king of Phaestos would be worth his service; would fate break him in his turn as Kenofer had so nearly been broken, or would he learn in time when to be humble and bend before the storm one cannot control?

Under the shade of the first trees they stopped. "But what

if you aren't chosen? There must be boys who aren't."
Kenofer asked. "How is it done?"

"I'm not sure, it's not something the guards are supposed to talk about afterwards, but I know it's better if you're strong, if you can run and climb and hunt. And I've still got five years to practise."

"And then afterwards, after you're chosen?"

"We are quartered in the palace. We stand guard over the king for the special festivals, there are the rites of the Mistress." He could not put it into words; it was all there running before his eyes like a gorgeous wall-painting, colour and dancing, admiring glances from the girls of the palace, the other young men of the guard laughing around him. At the end a place of honour in the court or even in the service of the High King at Knossos.

"You will make us a song? One we can sing after the Choosing, one that belongs just to our year?"

Kenofer followed him down the steep path. "Yes, you shall have your song. I must make a song of Phaestos for your father too." Five years; in that time he would have seen so much more and Kallisté would be no more than a grey ghost sleeping below the northern horizon, still and quiet like the dead who rested there. Why was it, then, that when he thought of a song for Phaestos the rhythm that welled up from the deep springs that he now knew were fed by his God had the anger and urgency of thunder? As he walked through into the courtyard of Myrtissos he was humming the small song for Theano that was half finished in his mind, but it was as if he was using it to keep something else from coming to the surface.

The will of his God would be done, that much he was sure of, whether it was through the singing of thunder, or of a marching song for Asterion. The prince called to him from the courtyard and the welcome and peace of Myrtissos were around him again.

88

PART TWO

The Return

9 ❧ The Shrine of the Mistress

Kenofer left the House of Singing Birds very early in the morning, when the air was still cool and hazy between the trees and the gold of the sun had not yet reached down into the plain from the higher slopes of Ida. He wanted to walk to Myrtissos, he needed the time to be quiet and to order his thoughts before he told those two whom with the Master he loved most the news that lay heavy on his heart; that had grown into such a burden during the last months that he could no longer carry it alone.

He walked fast until he had left the houses that climbed down the slopes of the Hill of the Kings behind him. The sun touched the silver leaves of the olives above the road and the air grew warm; it was still quiet with the early morning hush in which sounds carry a long way. A well-rope creaked at a farm hidden in the trees and high above on a bare hillside a goatherd was singing. Phaestos had been his home, and the House of Singing Birds the haven to which he always returned, for five years now, the five years that Geryon had spoken of at Myrtissos.

Those years had changed the young man who walked down the dusty road, and now he was the welcome and seemingly assured guest of kings across the Great Island and the sea beyond. Yet in his heart he was still often the bewildered boy who had played in the palace of Phaestos five years before. He had grown taller, but he was still slim, thinner-faced, swift-moving, reserved when he was not among close friends; reserved only until his hands touched his lyre.

He walked quickly with his head up, lost in his thoughts, until his sandal caught in a pot-hole in the road and he almost fell. He had not seen it. That brought him up short, shaken by more than the sudden stumble. How long—a year, or months only—would he still walk surely alone? He went on more slowly, his head bent. It had seemed, five years before, that a sword-blade had cut across his life, dividing him from so much that had been dear to him throughout his childhood, when he had been taken from Kallisté. And now his life was to be changed again and he found his thoughts turning northward with an ever deepening urgency. But through his own distress another voice was sounding, though the words were still indistinct. The years of his training with the Master had given him a skill and a sureness in interpreting emotion and making of it something that could be shared and understood. Even now as he walked this uncertainty nagged at the back of his mind like the first faint throbbings of toothache; then he came out from under the trees into a patch of bright sunlight that dazzled his eyes so that he had to stop and cover them with his hands.

At Myrtissos Theano too had been up for a long time, but still she was later than she had meant to be. Planning to wake early she had slept badly, woken at cock-crow and told herself that it was still night; besides, it had been difficult to get up without waking Aethra.

She had not been to the shrine so early before, and never alone; knowing where she was going made even the now familiar orchards of Myrtissos seem mysterious. On the lower slopes behind the house the apples and almonds and pomegranates grew close together, the ground between them already cracking with the heat of the beginning of summer. It was thick with dead leaves and straggling vetch and thistle plants straining up from the deep shade; a single vermilion pome-granate flower fallen from above lay at her feet like a star. The shrine was much higher up, deep in the cleft in the hills behind the house, and the path did not go there directly. It wound back and forth across the south-facing vine terraces and then became a donkey-track blown with dry droppings caught between the stones polished by passing hooves. Beyond the olives it belonged to the goatherds, and then on the bare hillside it led only to the Goddess.

Theano stopped on the last olive terrace to get her breath, because she had been climbing fast and her best flounced skirt made her hot even so early. The trees here were far older than the house, no longer single trunks, but sometimes broken circles of bark that looked like a group of old women huddled together for gossip. It would be hard to be sure one was alone, if so near the shrine of the Mistress one could be truly alone; her hands seemed cupped around the whole fruitful valley and the great house, where the first smoke from the bread-ovens was mingling with a trail of mist from the lower vineyards. It was time to hurry again.

She had her offerings wrapped in a cloth to hide them from her friend's inquisitive eyes; honey-cakes saved from yester-day's meal, and as many beads from her amethyst and crystal necklace as she had been able to slip off without its showing too much. And she had a stem of lilies that had lain broken from one of the pots outside Prince Geryon's room as she tiptoed out of the house, as though they had been left there on purpose. What she was going to pray about was the most serious thing that had happened to her since she came to Myrtissos and it was also the most private.

The shrine was at the head of the valley, not really a cave, more a deep niche in the grey orange-stained rock, as if great hands had reached in and torn it apart in a tattered hole like a rent in kneaded dough. There was a natural ledge inside that someone had plastered flat, and outside a pine-tree with a lightning-riven trunk that fluttered with the bleached rags and little trinkets that the country people brought. Inside on the ledge there were clay figures, pots on the floor, some already tipped on one side and broken, and the plaster horns still patched with red paint that showed it was a holy place. On the front of the ledge flies buzzed at the last of a saucer of honey standing on a wreath of dead roses; someone had been this way the day before. It was so different from the shrine her mother had served on Kallisté, and yet the offerings were the same. The hurt of her mother's death, that she had soothed and put to rest during the last five years, stirred again, but she pushed it down; that was not what she had come here to remember.

She did not notice the lock of hair, almost hidden by the dead flowers, until she had made her own offering, standing eyes closed and hands raised while she tried to get the words right. She had not said them alone before, and it made a difference, particularly when one was scared and churned up inside anyway with dreaming about Asterion and wondering what had happened to him during the last month in the mountains. It was also difficult, however much one was trying to be honest, to pray for someone's dream to come true when that would mean hardly seeing them for a year, particularly when one felt about them as she now did about Asterion, even if he was the prince's son. When at last she saw the hair she did not believe it at first—a long dark tress, wavy, with more spring to it than her own, cut unevenly across as if it had been sawn off with a knife. She heard his voice before she realized whose hair it was.

"The Mistress give you your prayer, Theano."

He had been behind the pine-tree. The sun was up now and the dazzle of it was in her eyes so that in the shadow she had not seen him, a slim dark boy, burnt brown by the sun, dusty, with his short kilt as torn as a goat-boy's. He had changed very little during the last years.

"But it's tomorrow, the Choosing, how did you get here?"

He came out from behind the tree and stood nearer her, while she searched his face eagerly but shyly for the changes the last month had brought.

"I shouldn't be, but we aren't far away. We don't really run all the way from Ida to the Hill of the Kings on the last morning. We have to rest and get cleaned up before the dancing. Why are you here, Theano?"

She did not answer that. "Then you're still . . .?"

"Yes. They call the feast tomorrow the Choosing, but we know already, last night they told us, the last twenty. I wanted to thank someone."

"And you came to Her here!"

"Yes. Why did you come, Theano?"

They were still in the shadow. He turned and went ahead of her a little way down the path, till the shrine was hidden and they came out into the sun with the prickly thyme already smelling of warmth and summer. Theano looked at the back of Asterion's head and wondered how she was ever to face his eyes. She had never been alone with him before. It had been one thing to adore and dream and giggle down in the great house, but he was four years older than she was, and a prince. And she had come to ask the Mistress for a blessing on his dream, not hers. Perhaps she had been answered twice over.

Asterion turned back to her in the sunlight. "It's good to see someone from home, I'd forgotten how good. Did my father's bitch have her puppies?"

"Yes, three. Two dark like her, and one ginger. It was the shepherd's dog after all."

He laughed. "They should be good trackers with that breeding." He looked at her properly then for the first time, and saw the best dress, wet at the hem with dew, and her shyness; a brown-haired girl nearly as tall as he, but not quite like the other girls in the house, with their quick dark eyes. But then she had been born on Kallisté.

He thought he knew the answer to his question now. "You came to pray because of the festival tomorrow!"

She nodded, and then, because her legs were trembling, sat down suddenly on a stone at the edge of the path.

"What was it like, in the mountains?" she asked. "Are you allowed to tell me?" He seemed so absorbed by what was happening to him that he accepted her interest without questioning it.

He did not answer her at first, partly wondering how to put into words the time spent high above the plain on the slopes of Ida with the others of his age, becoming no longer just the boys who had been born during the same few months, but the young men from whom the king's Summer Guard would be chosen. Those who were left after fate and the last contests, and who would go to the palace tomorrow.

"At first it was hard, worse than I had expected. It was cold at night so high up, and I didn't know that I could be so tired and still wake the next morning and climb and run. We were hungry too, till we learnt to be better hunters."

"You had to kill your own food?"

"Not all of it, but we only ate well when we had killed a deer or a boar. Those were the best days." He was silent again, seeing the firelight red on the circle of young faces, hearing the wind above in the high gullies among the firs, and the singing.

"After that it was mostly more like a game. Then the Choosing began. A boy from one of the farms fell and broke his arm, three got sick, partly that was how it happened; then some days you woke and someone else had left in the night. Three days ago the last contests started."

"We shall see you run past but not what happens after," said Theano. "And then you'll be away in the palace all those months."

"I suppose I shall." Getting there had been all that Asterion had thought of, all the last year and during the month of the

96

Choosing. He had hardly looked beyond that to the duties of the Summer Guard, the discipline, the training and the rites that must be performed. How would life be on the Hill of the Kings? He knew that all was not well from what he had overheard of his father's talk with close friends during the last years, but things were no worse than they had been for a long time and Asterion had pushed such thoughts away from him. And life would go on at Myrtissos; pretty Theano would laugh with the other girls and look after the little ones as she did now. They would all go on running a little wild because his grandmother was now dead and the aunt who was priestess to the house could not control the children. Still, Theano would be married soon. It all seemed as small and busy as the life of a beehive and as little to do with him.

Theano sat silent, seeing some of what he was thinking without the need of words. Because it was difficult to look Asterion in the face she glanced down past him into the valley that lay between the hill of Myrtissos and the long hog-back of scrub-covered rock that hid the Hill of the Kings. The road from the palace ran clear from the olive-groves below where she sat, a pale ribbon, dust still rising from the hooves of a flock of sheep being driven down from the foothills of Ida for the feasting tomorrow. At first the road was empty, then a man walked out of the haze, his shadow long before him.

Theano could see farther than most people. She stood up and shaded her eyes from the level rays of the sun.

"Who are you looking at?" Asterion turned to follow her gaze. "No, it's too far for me. Who is it?"

The man was walking steadily; he came another hundred paces before she was sure.

"It's my brother."

"Kenofer? Are you sure? But coming away from the palace —he'll be needed there tomorrow. What would bring him to Myrtissos today and on foot?"

"He always walks, didn't you know? He has a donkey for his robe and his lyre, but he says the rhythm of the hooves is wrong for thinking."

Asterion looked puzzled, but his mind was too full of other things to dwell for long on the strange habits of Kenofer the bard.

"He must have come just to talk. I must go. The Mistress grant us both our prayers."

It would be easier once he had loosed himself from this last link with home. Theano was looking straight at him now.

"Go in safety, today and tomorrow. Prince Geryon will tell us all that happens."

He went quickly, running up the track without looking back. Suddenly a partridge broke from cover at the edge of the path and clattered up into the sky. Fly right, the lucky side, prayed Theano, but the bird veered neither to left nor right but flew straight up over the hill towards the north. Perhaps it was not an omen from the Mistress after all.

Theano picked the burrs out of her skirt and looked back down at the road; her brother was almost below her now and looking up. She waved but he did not see her. She picked up her full skirts and ran down the hillside, trying to reach the big house before he arrived and anyone missed her. It would be bad enough if her friend Aethra found out where she had been, she must not know that Theano had spoken to Asterion. She was not sure if it was forbidden to talk to one of the Chosen and this was not the time to find out.

The stockyards and kitchen courtyard behind the house were full of the usual morning bustle, horses were being groomed and maids were carrying water from the well. She looked up at the high balcony on the first floor which faced this way, but it was empty and no one saw which way she had come.

Her brother had arrived before her; he was standing in the main courtyard talking to the prince, as she had expected.

Much as she loved him, Kenofer the bard, as he now was, was not someone one rushed to greet like an untrained puppy; after the last five years at the courts of kings he had acquired a courtier's dignity. She paused to get her breath and straighten the flounces on her long skirt, and then stood in the shade of the tall red pillars waiting to be noticed.

It seemed a long time ago, an earlier life, when they had been together on Kallisté. Theano had learned that to remember too much only brought back the pain, so she had taught herself to forget. She had been only nine when the welcome of Myrtissos was thrown round her like a warm cloak; here she was safe and happy among people who were fond of her. Tossing, sick and shocked speechless with grief in the bottom of the scout-boat which brought her south from the ruins of her home, she had not hoped for anything at all. All this had been given to her, and her brother alive, though no longer there each day to see and speak to and know properly.

She thought that he looked more like their father now, but it was hard to remember so far back. Kenofer was taller than many of the men of the Great Island and his hair was dark brown, not black, and straighter than theirs; he wore it tied back from his high forehead. The planes of his face and jaw had strengthened so that he could look grim, and indeed there was a hint of that in his expression now, so that she wondered what was troubling him, or if he had been ill and she had not heard. It seemed strange to see him talk to his friend and not smile.

Prince Geryon was only fifteen years the older but he looked more; heavily built, he was thickening towards middle age, and a severe fever had left him bald, which among his long-haired countrymen made him an arresting figure. Today he looked his full age, and there was something in his face that made her wonder if he was going to be ill again.

With one hand on the prince's arm, Kenofer was speaking urgently. It was Geryon who saw her first.

"Look, she's here."

But they could not have been talking about her! Now Theano could run forward into her brother's arms, and then remember her manners in time to curtsy to the prince. Kenofer held her off at arm's length as he always did to look at her properly, with the smile that she loved twitching the corners of his mouth.

"Come," said the prince. "We shall be quieter in my room."

10 ❧ Theano Decides

Kenofer, his hand still on her shoulder, took Theano through into the men's hall. The prince called for a servant to close the folding doors which led into the courtyard and open those facing east up the valley behind the house. It was sunny and quiet. Kenofer sat down on the bench that ran round the room and drew her down beside him; Prince Geryon stood a little way off, looking down at them. Theano, alarmed by the unfamiliar room and the way the two men were looking at her, had a sudden feeling of being trapped.

Kenofer saw her uneasiness and understood it; he had not realized that she was so quick to sense emotion. He could see that Geryon was still trying to comprehend what he had told him so hurriedly outside in the courtyard. He must try to be more gentle with Theano, but it was going to be difficult.

"I've come to tell you something—no, two things—that it may be hard for you to hear. Will you listen to me to the end, and try to understand?" His hands were twisting on his knees, the long fingers plaiting together. What he had to say would be as hard for him as for her.

"Theano, do you remember two years ago when my eyes were bad?"

"The autumn when you were here for two months because they were too sore for you to travel?"

"Yes. I told myself then that it still came from the dust after the earthshaking. You remember how most of us from Kallisté had sore eyes at first and couldn't stop coughing?"

She nodded her head, not wanting to think about it.

"It was more than the dust, and during the winter it's been coming back. There is a priestess at Knossos who is skilful in these things. Last month I went to her and made an offering, and she examined me. Theano, I am going blind. Already I can only see clearly straight ahead of me, and it will get worse."

There was one of those silences that last only for a moment but divide what has gone before from what comes after like the slamming of a door.

Theano shivered in the sunny room and her own voice sounded small and flat to her. "I waved just now from the hillside above the road and you didn't see me." That was not what she should have said, but no other words came.

"I'm sorry, Theano. I have had a little time to understand what the priestess told me, what it will mean. It is coming very suddenly to you; please try to understand. There are others who have the God's gift of music in their hands who are blind, but with them it is usually the blindness which comes first and the music after as a special gift. And they do not travel the roads of the Great Island alone. When I am blind that will not be possible for me either."

His tightly clasped hands were still now. She put out her own to touch them and his fingers took hers, strong and warm.

Kenofer opened his mouth to speak again but no words came; he looked up in despair at Prince Geryon. The big man came and sat down across from them, where he could see them both.

"Theano, you have lived with us at Myrtissos for five years, you have given us back in love what you have received in care. I thought I should soon be finding a husband for you as I shall for my niece Aethra. But I think now that the God of Kallisté who saved the hands of Kenofer for his own purposes has reached out and touched you too. I think there is a new road before you. No, don't be frightened, just listen to Kenofer."

Kenofer had released her hands and was leaning back against the wall, painted like a garden with craggy little hills and trees and lilies like the ones that swayed in pots on the terrace. Theano found that she was looking at them and not at Kenofer's face.

"For the moment I can see well enough for most things. When the darkness grows thicker I shall need other eyes to see for me and lead me up the steps of strange palaces. I shall need a shoulder I can put my hand on. My God has led me to you. Once I promised you that when you needed me I would always come. Now I can only ask you to come to me."

She understood now, and it was as if she had felt the breath of this coming an hour before when near the shrine the bird had flown north. The omen had been for her after all. But she was not ready to answer yet.

"If your God saved you on Kallisté why doesn't he let you keep your eyes?" she asked. And why could he not come and live quietly with her at Myrtissos when his sight failed? But she knew the answer to that without asking; the man who could accept this new fate so meekly would be no longer her brother.

"Don't you think I've asked the same thing myself," he said. "I think that my God has many different voices. Theano, he did not destroy a whole island to save my hands for himself, but my gift and my fate are bound up with him and with Kallisté. What he gave to me has sometimes been heavy to bear, but at least I know that blind or seeing I shall still play. For the rest it is a problem I must solve for myself. Theano, now I must ask you, will you leave Myrtissos and come with me? I will not force you, because you will find such a wandering life difficult and strange, and because the first thing I must ask of you will be the most difficult. Later I hope that we shall travel as I have before to the palaces of many kings, but first will you come with me to Kallisté?"

"Back home? Why? Oh no . . ."

It was as if the ground had opened before her and thrown her down into a darkness echoing with all her oldest fears. Theano had buried Kalisté and her dead mother deep in her heart, but it had only been possible because she had known that she would not see the ruins of her shattered home again.

Watching her closely Kenofer was no longer sure that his sister was listening, yet he must go on, he must try to explain what he did not really understand himself.

"That was the second thing I had to tell you, first about my eyes and then about Kallisté. You know that during the last two years some of the men of the island have gone back. Of course the town is still mostly in ruins, but it has seemed that the anger of the God has passed and Kallisté may begin to be a home again—at least for some of us. Isander is there, planning the clearing of the rubble and the new building that must be done; he went two months ago. With the knowledge of what was coming to me I knew that I must see Kallisté again, one last time—while I still could."

"But you wouldn't need to stay there long?" Perhaps she could bear that, a few hours, two or three days, and then away. Dimly Theano was aware that the horror of darkness waiting for her brother was far greater than her own childish fear of returning to the place where she had been in such terror, yet that was what was filling her own mind and blotting out everything else.

Theano had drawn far enough away to be out of reach of the touch of Kenofer's hands. The dark troubled man sitting so close seemed a stranger; how could she leave Myrtissos to go with him? She turned to the prince for help. Geryon was looking at her. There was gentleness in his warm brown eyes and understanding in the big mouth, but she could not doubt what he would say or do if she refused his friend now. Kenofer had asked her a question, but there was no choice open before her. If she did not leave her new home to go with him it would not seem a home any longer. She would live there with the knowledge that she had refused her help to the person she loved most. Both men were silent, knowing they had already said all that could be said. It was for her to speak now and still the words would not come.

It was too much to accept all at once. She had prayed for Asterion, going out from Myrtissos tomorrow to a new life, not knowing that she would leave as soon as he. Had the Mistress answered her own prayer, even in this strange way, as quickly as his God had answered Kenofer? They were waiting and she understood from the new deep lines on Kenofer's face how much it had already cost him to come to her and put his future in her hands.

Her voice came out with a catch in it. "When must we leave?"

Geryon sat back and Kenofer drew in his breath. "Today, Theano. I must be back at the Hill of the Kings before dusk; there will be feasting tonight and again tomorrow after the Choosing."

"We must go through the old customs for the sake of our children," said Geryon.

But Theano was beginning to understand something new. She would be at the Hill of the Kings tomorrow, on the day of the Choosing, and the thought of that blinded her to anything else. She would be there, she would see Asterion, that would carry her through the next hours at least, before the numbness wore off and she understood fully what had happened. Then the panic that comes over all women flooded over her.

"I've never been further than the far side of the plain all the time I've been here. What clothes shall I need for your palaces and journeys?"

Prince Geryon roared with laughter and kissed her. "My sister can decide that, we will go to her. But you must be ready to leave two hours after noon."

Theano made a small curtsy and walked out of the room with her head up, but outside in the courtyard it was different. Not waiting for Geryon, she ran up the stairs to the women's rooms, picking up her skirts as if a wild cat was after her. She was not sure if she wanted to be sick or to cry, but whichever it was had better be done in the small room she still shared with Aethra.

Her friend, guided by the rumours that were already flying round the house, had been waiting for her in the courtyard, but Theano passed her without noticing. Aethra climbed the stairs more slowly and closed the door of their room behind her.

Kenofer's hand on his arm stopped the prince so that he did not follow Theano from the room after all. The younger man was shaking as if with fever; the prince steadied him and they walked together on to the terrace.

In a voice that he could not yet fully control, Kenofer said, "I didn't think she would come, not so quickly. I hoped, and I knew I must ask her, but I didn't see how she would find the strength to do it."

"Women are stronger than men, stronger in many ways," said the prince. "She will come, though she thinks it will break her heart, because she loves you. And then she will find that her heart is not broken after all. When will you leave Phaestos?"

"Soon, when the feast of the Choosing is over. I have this feeling in me that the birds must have when they fly north over the island in the spring. I too must go north and it must be now."

"Have you had a sending from the God?"

"No. I don't know, not that I can be sure of." Kenofer spoke very quietly.

"Long farewells are the most difficult, I know that," said the prince. "But we shall see you again. After Kalliste the time will come when you will turn south back to the Great

Island, both of you. I don't make such a friend as you to lose again so quickly."

"Of course," said Kenofer, and then wondered why in this moment the memory of Phormio should come back to him. Phormio the first friend and the first to be lost; was that a pattern that would be repeated again and again in his life? Must every person and every thing that he loved be taken from him? But no, he was tired, this mood would pass once the journey was begun and the partings behind him.

"You never made me my song of Phaestos," said Geryon, suddenly feeling how short the time was when Kenofer would be there to answer and to sing.

"No more I did! But I've made Asterion and his friends their marching song, and perhaps after all it has become a song for Phaestos and not only for them. I hope he will like it. I suppose it is certain that he is among the Chosen?"

Geryon laughed. "Asterion? The very summit of the White Mountain would have been thrown down about our ears by now if that hadn't happened. When will you sing the song, Kenofer?"

"Tomorrow at the feast of the Choosing." The young man beat out a marching rhythm with one hand on the parapet of the terrace and sang softly.

> *Though wind shakes the forest*
> *The mountain is steadfast.*
> *White Mountain, Mount Ida,*
> *Our strength is like yours.*
> *Though children fear thunder*
> *No more are we children,*
> *Together, together*
> *We march strong as men.*

"You have made them a song of thunder—and yet, yes, I think Asterion will be well pleased."

"I can only make what the God sends," said Kenofer,

turning away from the view of the mountain that he could no longer clearly see. "Yes, there is thunder there, even more when I play the lyre part."

Almost it seemed that he felt the pavement begin to shift under his feet and he heard the distant thunder of Kallisté. Before the moon was full again he would be climbing his own mountain with Theano.

11 ⚶ The Hill of the Kings

Aethra looked across from the pile of belongings she was making on her own bed to Theano crouched shivering on hers.

"If you mind as much as this, why didn't you tell your brother you wouldn't go? But to see the palace, and Knossos and the whole island! Theano, are you sure he wouldn't take me instead?"

"If only he would." For a moment Theano shook herself loose from the misery that had wrapped itself around her like a dark fog. "But no, he wouldn't. It's only because I'm his sister that he can bear to ask me. Kenofer could hire a train of servants or even take a pupil with him if he wanted to. But, Aethra, is this going to last all my life? Will it go on for ever?"

Aethra put down the sandal she was holding, sat on her friend's bed and put her arms about her. Theano stayed stiff and unyielding, still locked away beyond the reach of her friend's easy reassurance. Aethra was the daring one, quick to laugh or to stop crying, small and merry like so many of the girls of the Great Island.

Theano pulled herself gently away and curled back into the corner of the bed, looking round the tiny room which had been hers for most of the last five years. It was still cool, for the high square window faced north. The sun was overhead now, it was nearly noon and all she could see was a patch of gilded blue; a bird darted across it and was gone. The smell of the last haymaking came from the slopes above the house.

The pinky-red paint below the dado half-way up the walls was shabby, chipped where their beds had banged against it during their rougher games; the window-sill and the chest-top were cluttered with special stones and wild flowers dying in pots and old dolls. She would not sleep here again. It would be a different Theano who came back to Myrtissos, if she ever came. Why must it be Theano, content in the new home she loved, that the will of a half-known God was drawing out from the shelter of her childhood?

There was a step outside in the passage; Theano slid off the bed and straightened her full skirts before the Lady of Myrtissos, Aethra's aunt, came into the room. She was small and plump, with a high colour, always a little out of touch with what was going on because she never listened to what anyone said. But it was she who served the house shrine of the Mistress, and as its priestess she had considerable authority. She took in the untidy room at a glance.

"You haven't finished? Then a maid must do it. Come, it's time. You too, Aethra, it will do you no harm to show proper reverence for once."

As she led the way from the room the woman changed from the familiar aunt of all the children in the house, related by blood or not, to the priestess of the Mistress. Her feet seemed to glide under her full skirts, sewn with little flowers of gold that tinkled when she walked. Silently, one behind the other, the girls followed her.

She led them through her own room to the small bathroom beyond. Her maids were already there and the earthenware bathtub was pulled away from the wall. Outside someone was playing a tune on a double flute, the notes running down again and again in the same broken scale. In silence the maids undressed Theano and she knelt in the bath, her face hidden in her hands, while they poured water over her.

"Her hair, my lady?" whispered the oldest maid.

"No, there isn't time."

The pouring stopped; the water had been warm and the room as well, but Theano felt cold as midwinter as she was dried with linen cloths and dressed again in her best everyday dress for the journey. The priestess arranged her hair herself, combing it into small curls at the brow and twining the side locks up on the crown with coloured ribbons.

Outside the flute still played and there was the hushed murmur of people waiting. With the same gliding walk the priestess led Theano and the other women of the house down the steps to the courtyard and to the door of the shrine on the south side.

It was dark and crowded in the little room. Theano could hardly see the clutter of small things, dedicated over the years like those in the shrine at the head of the valley, only richer. Here on the altar shelf there was a tall bronze-headed axe, set into a socket, its double blades shaped like the lotus flowers of a necklace the priestess wore, and below it a tiny ivory figure of the Mistress, her arms wreathed in snakes. The flute played and the women sang, as, in a way Theano was too dazed to understand, the Mistress sent her out cleansed and protected from her home to what lay before her on the road with Kenofer.

Theano did not walk to the Hill of the Kings. Prince Geryon rode ahead, driving himself in his own chariot with Kenofer by his side, while she followed behind with the captain of the escort, a silent man she had known ever since she came to the house, who left her to think her own thoughts while he kept his attention on avoiding what he could of the dust thrown up by the horses ahead.

She had not often been in a chariot before; it felt as if her old life was being pulled away from her faster and faster as the horses took the curve at the bottom of the hill, below the spur where she had seen Kenofer that morning, and the house with Aethra and the other women waving was out of sight. All that she was taking with her was in a basket at her feet.

The road ran down through the barley fields, past a cluster of the small houses of the country people, and then under the olives that flowed in a great sweep like a winter-flooding river across the floor of the valley between Myrtissos and the dry slopes that still hid the Hill of the Kings.

Above to her left, where the ground was higher, ran the track that led down from the foothills to the north and the mountain peaks, hidden from here, where snow still lay in the gullies. That was the way the boys would come tomorrow. Then she remembered Asterion again for the first time since morning. Who knew when she would see him after, but at least she would see him tomorrow at the Choosing, and that had been beyond her wildest hope.

Did she love him? Theano had thought so, she had thought of little else during the last winter and spring. That was when she had gone shy of him, no longer able to talk as she did with the other boys of the household, but making it her business to sit where she could see him, and touch what he had touched. He was handsome certainly, dark and quick with an air of confidence all his own, but other boys in the house were as good-looking, brown and lightfooted in their short kilts, their long wavy hair flying loose. And Asterion was the only son of a prince, it had never really mattered if she had loved him or not, not for anything that could have come of it.

This morning at the shrine had been the first time she had spoken to him for so long, and yet after the first shock it had been easier than she would have expected. But that could not mean anything on this day when she was being swept along by a power she could not control. Now the problem of Asterion, about whom she had never done more than dream, was less important than the unknown palace ahead, and the unknown house where she would sleep that night. Kenofer might be her brother but would he still understand the things that frightened her?

The road swung westwards below the shoulder of the

barren hill. Now the sea, with the sun low above it, glittered to the west at the end of the plain and the long hog's-back of the Hill of the Kings lay ahead, fringed with orchards and villas, the old palace high on the eastern crest. Through the swirling dust Theano saw terraces with red-painted pillars and the topmost roofs jagged against the paling sky with the giant sacred horns that edged them. Then they were under the trees again.

When the chariot ahead stopped they were on the saddle on the ridge to the west of the palace, which was out of sight from there. The road was crowded with people coming up from the town that spread down the southern slopes, to see the guests arriving for the first banquet of the Choosing. This was the way the boys would come, at the last. Kenofer got down from the chariot ahead and walked back to her.

"Come, I'll take you home, my home. It isn't far from here."

She got down stiffly and the guard handed out her basket. Kenofer, with one flick of his expressive hands, summoned a boy from the crowd to carry it and led the way across the southern slope of the hill. Before long he turned right into a narrow lane between high walls, the ground carved into the comfortable ruts that would last all summer. It was quieter here away from the crowds. Kenofer strode ahead, not looking back, and Theano followed, holding up her long skirt from the dust. She could hear the boy panting behind.

Kenofer stopped at a gate on the right-hand side where a large house was built against the slope of the hill. The door stood open. He turned to the boy.

"Wait!"

Theano waited too outside the house till he came back with his hands full of small green pears, still warm from the tree. The boy put down the basket, grinned his gratitude and scampered off. Kenofer turned then to Theano, saw how she was drooping wearily in the gateway, took her hand and smiled.

"This is the House of Singing Birds."

She had heard about it for so long and wondered about the Master who lived there, but now she hung back, almost too weary for new places and people.

"Come on," he said. "The Master is waiting to greet you."

He led her through into the courtyard. The house lay beyond it, high, with square windows and painted beams. On the eastern side of the courtyard, where the sinking sun still cast a warm light on the whitewashed walls, an older man sat on a stone bench under a pomegranate tree. Theano had a quick impression of dark and light and glossy leaves, and then all her attention was fixed on the man smiling at her.

"Come here, child." The hand that beckoned was thin and veined, and trembled when he raised it from his knee.

Theano sank into as deep a curtsy as she could manage with legs that were still shaking from the chariot ride, and then sat on the stool he pointed to.

First the man spoke to Kenofer. "Yes, go up to your room, it's time you made ready. We unpacked your baggage, so your singing robe is fit to wear. I will take care of Theano."

Kenofer smiled and went quickly into the house. Then it was quiet in the sunny courtyard and there was a great air of peace. Somewhere inside a lyre was being played, the Master had known her name, and she was expected. She had imagined herself perhaps already at the palace, awed and frightened by the unfamiliar bustle; she was glad that there were still a few hours more in which she could try to understand the changes that one day had brought to her life.

"You will learn," said the Master, "when you are with Kenofer, that before he is to play, if it can be managed he must have a time alone. Of course it's easy when he is here with us, where he has his own room."

"I always wondered why he lived here with you and not at Myrtissos. I suppose that's why."

"Yes, partly. Theano, yesterday Kenofer told me for the

first time what the priestess had said about his eyes. At first I was too moved to be able to give him help and guidance, and then it seemed that he needed none. The plan was fixed in his head to go to Myrtissos to you. I told him that he was asking a great deal—to leave your home at a moment's notice, to go with someone who is now almost a stranger to you. For although he is your brother, since you came to the Great Island you have seen him seldom. I doubted if you would come, but you are here. I think the Mistress has guided your heart."

Then Theano found that she could talk more easily to this frail, gentle man who sat so still, with the soft voice that held the traces of old melodies, than even to Aethra at home.

"I don't know why I came and I'm frightened. But when my brother asked me Prince Geryon was there, and I think I was too proud to show how frightened I was. I think that's the only reason I'm here, and it isn't really enough."

The Master smiled. "At least it's an honest reason, which is a good beginning. And I understand well that Prince Geryon is difficult to refuse. The well-being of his friend is dear to him, it always has been. He would pluck out one of his own eyes for Kenofer if it was possible, but he has always known that your brother must be free to live the only way he can."

He shifted in his seat and Theano saw that he had only been so still because his hands had been tightly clasped upon his knee; without that they trembled like birch-leaves in a breeze. Looking at them she could not imagine that they had ever held a lyre.

The man noticed what she was looking at and smiled again. "Yes, I too have paid my price to the God. It is more than two years now since I could play."

"Are you really the Master who came to Kallisté and played at the palace of Aglauros?" Theano asked.

"I am. Does it seem so strange?"

A servant had come to the house door and seemed to be waiting for orders.

"Yes, we will eat here," said the Master. "Our guest must be thirsty and she will be more at ease when she has eaten."

The food which the man brought was very simple, but at the sight of it, Theano, who had thought that she was too tired to eat, found she was hungry after all. There was fresh bread, and cheese, and a plate of lettuce and salad herbs, and a bowl of the small pears. The wine came in a jar already mixed with cool well-water; the servant poured the first cups and then left them to serve themselves.

The Master ate very little, and drank only one cup. When he saw that Theano had all she wanted he began to talk again. He told her the story of his first meeting with Kenofer and Theano began to understand for the first time something of the awe and respect with which the skill of the unknown boy from Kallisté had been received.

"It was beyond anything that could have been expected, that a boy with so little training should play like that," said the old man with his beautiful thoughtful smile. "It was as if a light was shining from behind him, through him."

The last of the sun's glow went from the wall above them as it dipped below the hill that lay between the town and the sea. Theano, finishing her second pear, thought of the light going out behind Kenofer's eyes, and for the first time began to understand a little of the darkness that lay ahead for him. That morning she had been distressed to leave her home, now she could begin to comprehend the greater loss that would come to him.

Watching her closely, the Master guessed her thoughts. "The power will still be there in his hands," he said. "I knew that first day that he would be the greatest of us all."

"Greater than you?"

For the first time he laughed. "Thank you, child, and you have never heard me play! Yes, Kenofer and I have different gifts. He draws his music from a very deep place. My hands were skilled and I could lay my own soul before those who heard me, but Kenofer leads men to see more deeply into their own hearts and minds."

Then Kenofer himself came out of the house in his long bard's robe of blue linen embroidered with white and yellow and purple across the shoulders and round the fringed hem. Holding his lyre in the crook of his arm he looked down at them and smiled.

"I see that you are already friends. Theano, you're tired, sleep while you can. Don't stay awake for me."

Theano got up, wondering where their room was, but her brother had already forgotten her, standing talking quietly with his old friend. A cheerful-looking man beckoned to her from the doorway and she followed him into the house.

"Tonight, and then only one more day," said Kenofer. "Why do I feel so uneasy, like a child with a difficult task to complete who will be punished if he doesn't get it right?"

The Master looked thoughtfully up at him. "It is better to give up quickly things that will be dragged away by force if we cling to them. But you want to go, well, it's only natural. You won't rest till you've seen Kallisté, with Theano. She's a good child."

"Yes," Kenofer answered, but his mind was already running ahead to the feasting that night and the songs he would sing.

After he had gone the old man sat a little longer in the cool of the little courtyard, thinking of the two of them. Kenofer had been a complicated person to deal with even as a boy, even before the darkness that now threatened him; yet it might be that from Theano's simplicity he would find the strength to live through the days that lay ahead.

12 ⚕ The Choosing

Theano woke once, very late, in a small room at the back of the house. Kenofer must just have come in. The full moon of the Choosing was bright on the wall, and by its light she saw him standing by the bed, his hands raised to loosen the gold clasp that held back his long hair. The sleeves of his robe swooped like birds' wings making shadows across the wall. Theano turned her back to him and pulled the cover closer against the night chill. She heard bedstrings creak as he lay down and then the room was quiet again except for the steady rhythm of his breathing. Before she slept she thought of Asterion not far away in the foothills, perhaps lying awake for the last time under the open sky.

There were voices below in the courtyard and outside in the lane before dawn. Theano woke confused and still tired, stretching out and feeling a wall on the wrong side of the bed. Kenofer was already partly dressed although his rest had been short. She sat up holding the cover round her.

"Good, you're awake! Can you do your hair yourself? We must be at the palace early or we shan't get through the crowds. Come down to the courtyard when you're ready."

It was the first time she had ever dressed alone, and her long hair was difficult to manage without Aethra's advice, but she did the best she could, and walked self-consciously down the stairs, holding up her flounced blue skirts. Kenofer was standing by the well in the dawn light, drinking a cup of milk. Theano dropped him a small curtsy.

"Will this do, it's the best dress I have?" she asked.

"Yes, I saw it yesterday, but that time there were burrs in the hem!" His smile was suddenly warm and familiar, the one she remembered from childhood.

"Come here. Now, turn round. Something isn't quite right." Theano felt his hands touch her hair, rearranging the long curls caught up to the crown at the back. His touch was gentle and firm, and she found that she wanted to lean back against his hand like a kitten being stroked, as a small girl will with a much loved brother. But the Kallisté where that had happened was so long ago.

"Is that too tight? Good, now you'll do. Eat quickly and then we must go."

As he led her down the lane she saw the first glint of gold from the rising sun touch the higher roofs of the town. People were already moving eastwards in a steady stream towards the crest of the ridge and the paved way to the palace. Kenofer held his lyre in the crook of his arm to protect it from the crowd.

"Now, keep close to me, here and all day. No one will bother you if you're with me, but neither a crowd nor a palace is a very safe place for a girl from the country alone."

"What's going to happen?" Theano asked, hurrying to keep up with Kenofer's long strides.

"It will have begun already, in the palace, the first rites, but those are for the king and the priestesses alone. The boys will probably come about two hours after sunrise. You know which way?"

They had reached the point where they had left the chariots the evening before. North across a narrow valley lay the bare hillside with a cleft which marked the track from the mountains. Myrtissos lay somewhere behind in the deeply shadowed foothills. Theano raised her eyes and saw snow in the gullies of the peaks of Ida high above. Kenofer followed her gaze.

"They say the snow is still deep this year."

"But you can . . ."

She saw the corner of his mouth twist. "No, Theano, I can't, not now. I can hardly see across the first valley! But you can see it."

One pace behind him, Theano waited till the hot colour had gone from her face before she asked, "What happens when the boys come into the palace?"

"They are brought into the great courtyard, and there the last of the rites takes place and the dancing. Then they are named, and their fathers stand sponsor for them before the king. The Summer Guard must come from families that are known and held in honour."

"Oh!" Theano caught hold of his free hand. They had come round the corner of the hill and now the western face of the palace was before them, towering in galleries three stories high above the portico and the great staircase that led to the inner courtyard. Already a crowd was waiting below the steps and the high balconies were a sea of faces.

Kenofer kept hold of her hand and led her round to the right of the main stairway. "No, we don't go that way. There's a lower door for the likes of us."

Theano doubted what he said for she had already noticed how his face seemed to be known by everyone and how the crowd had parted and made way. It was dark and close in the narrow corridors and twisting steps up which he led her. The lower parts of the palace seemed thronged with perfumed shadows who passed laughing, tinkling with gold and amethyst and crystal beads.

Then a stair brought them to the lowest balcony on the east side of the courtyard. It was large, like a market-place, at least forty paces long and paved with stone. Between the red painted pillars of the arcade guards were posted to keep the centre clear, but above on the balconies that faced inwards the crowds were even thicker and more brilliant. Here the ladies of the court were waiting, gay as a flower-garden and noisy as a cage of birds. The sun was already sweeping down the high walls into the courtyard.

It had moved back half across the paving when the roar of sound from the hillside outside warned those within that the boys were coming. The hour that she had stood, leaning far over the balcony, seemed to have gone by in a moment. Now, suddenly, she remembered why she was there and what was going to happen just below her. Asterion was coming, and she would see him. Then there was a last moment of panic that he had fallen, that he was ill, that for some unimaginable reason he would not come.

The roar was almost inside the palace, the ladies on the terraces buzzed and chattered. Then there was a hush. From the portico that led out to the great stairway came the sound of chanting and the wail of double flutes; the priestesses swept into sight.

There was a stir directly opposite, under the arcade where the doorway of the palace shrine was still in deep shadow. The king came slowly out to stand between two pillars, a tall, narrow-faced man, very dark, a high crown of golden lilies on his head. Then Theano saw that a woman as gorgeously dressed led the priestesses.

"The queen," breathed Kenofer into her ear in the sudden hush, peering down into the brilliant dazzle below.

The head of the procession curved round, walking almost a circuit of the courtyard to finish before the lonely, waiting figure of the king. Then the women parted to left and right, standing on either side of him, and the music stopped as the boys came in, pacing two by two.

There were twenty of them, much of a height, dark hair caught back, the sun warm on bare brown skin gleaming with sweat. The running was over but their chests still heaved with the effort of it, and of walking in time on legs that still felt like lead. They were all dressed alike, in short cutaway kilts of the dark palace red.

She could not see him. They were so alike that Theano could not see him, and then she saw why; Asterion was already below her, he had been one of the first pair.

They stood in rows behind the priestesses, spread across the whole length of the courtyard, still, their hands at their sides, facing the king. Then the singing began again, first the priestesses and then the deeper voices of the boys answering them. From below out of sight under the colonnade came the beating of a drum to lead them. The boys began to sway gently, together, the movement rippling down the spaced lines. Theano thought of barley blown silky and dappled by the wind and understood that this was what the singing had been telling her. The young men of the Summer Guard were the new harvest of the people.

Then they danced, wheeling in lines, the young priestesses threading their way between them. The drum-beat quickened. The long curls of the girls swung out and their full skirts whirled; the boys were panting. Asterion passed below Theano, his face set, utterly absorbed by what he was doing.

And there was movement too on the high balconies, a surging as the crowd swayed with them, and cried out, drowning the singing while the only still point in the colour and pattern was the upright figure of the king, motionless except that the golden lilies of his crown stirred in the wind of the dance.

Kenofer had been watching Theano's excitement, not the scene below. The dazzle and the brilliance of it hurt his eyes; he had seen it before and now all the ritual of the court of Phaestos seemed no more to him than a wind blowing among the bright short-lived flowers that lost their colour with the setting sun. Yet in spite of himself he had been moved when the music began. The drumming was insistent, breaking in through his confused thoughts. But the message for him was quite different from that for the dancers below. It came with a force as overwhelming as a great wave breaking over his head and dragging him down into a choking darkness.

Theano realized that Kenofer beside her was gasping, almost crying under his breath. Suddenly she was frightened, it was all too much, she wanted it to stop. She pressed close against him and felt his arm come round her strongly, holding her so close that she could feel that he was trembling, not swaying with the rest of the crowd. Then she twisted her head and looked up into his face. Kenofer's eyes were shut; whatever it was that was moving him so deeply, it was not what she could see below in the courtyard.

The pace of the drum-beats slackened, the noise ebbed so that the panting of the dancers sounded louder than the music. The girls parted to left and right, disappearing between the pillars, and the boys were left back in the places from which they had started, down on one knee, their heads bent.

Asterion was far away across the courtyard. Theano watched the boy directly below her, the long drops of sweat running down his bare back and making dark stains on his kilt. Then he slowly raised his head, pushed back the dark hair from his face, stood, and faced inwards. Out from the shadows beside the king came two priestesses carrying a round pottery altar with short legs. They set it down in front of the shrine. It was like one Theano had seen at Myrtissos, only much bigger, with many little hollows pressed into the clay all round the rim. She knew what was going to happen now.

Sure enough, the girls were coming back, each carrying one of the tall pointed vases that were used only in the ritual of the Mistress. The young men followed them towards the altar. Each in turn bowed low, took a handful of the seeds and grains they contained and filled one of the hollows, till the fruit of all that grew in the plain lay before the king; the fruits of the labour of the people and the fruit of their bodies. The king spread his hands in blessing and the priestesses cried out all together, a high call that could be heard even beyond the palace. From outside on the hillside came an answering roar.

The altar was carried away, the women disappeared between the pillars again and the king smiled for the first time and spread out his arms towards the waiting young men. Kenofer's grasp slackened round Theano's shoulders and she drew a deep breath. What she had seen had moved her and frightened her in a way she was too confused to understand, but now came the moments that were all joy and pride for her and for everyone who had kin waiting below to be named to the king.

The order of the boys had changed and Asterion would be among the last. The first came forward to stand very alone before the king; the muscles of his thighs tightened with the effort of remaining motionless while a herald cried, "Who names his son before the king?"

An officer of the royal guard stepped forward and cried out his own name and that of his son. The boy knelt to kiss the king's hand; then on either side a captain stepped forward. One gave the father a shield to give to his son and the other put a sword-belt into the king's hands. The boy stood stiffly while the king swung it round his waist, fastening the clasp; then his father gave him the shield. The boy stood for a moment longer and then swung round and stood facing the people. A shout went up; Theano saw his glance go quickly to one end of a balcony where there were voices he knew. His mouth twitched and steadied, and then he moved to one side, the first of a long double line that spread across the courtyard as one by one the boys came forward to the king and the ceremony was repeated. With those shields and swords they would dance again at the next full moon before the Mistress's shrine.

Their fathers were guards and courtiers and landowners from the farms across the plain; once there was a pause as a man older than the others came forward on the arm of an elder son, leaning on a stick, and for a few long heartbeats a boy waited to hear his name called.

Theano had seen where Prince Geryon stood to one side, a little clear of the colonnade where other men waited for their turn to come. She wondered what it meant to him to see his own son honoured but yet by a court which he himself had left in anger. The boy before Asterion rose to his feet and turned to his father for his shield. The moment Theano had been waiting for had come.

Asterion stood alone and Prince Geryon moved forward. Then she felt that Kenofer at her side was shaking as if he had a fever; Theano dragged her eyes away from the small bright figures below her. As the herald's voice cried out the familiar words Kenofer turned towards her, his face grey and beaded with sweat.

"Don't you feel it?"

She took his arm to steady him and felt his trembling go right through her, like the shivering of a tree waiting for the last blow of the axe.

"Kenofer, feel what?"

She glanced quickly down. Asterion was on one knee, dark head bowed.

Kenofer dragged his gaze round to follow where she looked; he blinked and put a hand to his eyes as if to clear his sight.

"Who is it?"

Geryon below answered for her. "Asterion son of Geryon, under the king lord of Myrtissos."

Kenofer groped back with his hand to the pillar beside him and leaned his head against it, eyes closed; below Asterion turned to face the people, his face alight with excitement. The gold hilt of his new sword flashed in the sun and a shout went up from the crowd, louder than they had given the others, as if they had sensed something special about this, the last of the guard.

Asterion turned sharply on his heel and took his place at the end of the front rank and Geryon moved back into the crowd. Theano turned to Kenofer.

"What is it, are you ill?"

Her brother's teeth were chattering, he pushed the lyre into her hands.

"Take it, or I shall drop it. Theano, is it over?"

She glanced down. The guard were marching off towards the lower entrance to the courtyard. "Yes, I think so. But what . . .?"

"Don't be frightened, I'm not ill. But Theano, I didn't know I should need you so much, so soon."

"Tell me what I can do."

13   A Song for the Chosen

The lyre still under her arm, Theano guided Kenofer down the narrow stairs; he seemed to be walking blind. They came out into the courtyard, crowded now with courtiers and palace servants coming down from the upper galleries.

"The north-eastern corner, there'll be a guard. I must have time to be still, and there's only one place in the palace that will be quiet today," he said.

Sure enough a guard was posted at the entrance to a corridor more splendid than any she had yet seen, painted with a frieze of hunting lions. When he saw Kenofer he stepped aside and let them pass without a word. At the end on the right a doorway led into a small courtyard, like the one at home at Myrtissos. Pillars and folding doors led through to what looked like private apartments, but other than a servant waiting in the shade there was no one about.

In the sudden quiet and coolness Kenofer already looked more like himself; he led her across to the bench that ran round the two shady sides. Theano sat down beside him and waited. A bird sang above them in a wicker cage and the petals from a yellow climbing rose in a pot beside her blew across the smooth paving of the courtyard. She looked down at the lyre she still held; it was the first time that she had touched it. The citrus wood was polished with care and use to the sheen of a bird's breast, but the faint lines of earlier mendings still showed. As she turned it the wind which spiralled down to blow the petals made the strings hum softly.

Kenofer heard the sound and turned his head to look at her, wondering how to explain something that was beyond even his own understanding. And Theano herself had for the moment forgotten Asterion; her entire concern now was with the strange, powerful, vulnerable young man beside her. Something more was the matter than the troubles she already knew, and however was she—already at sea in the strange world of the palace—to know how to help him?

"Where are we?" she asked.

"These are the apartments of the crown prince, Laomedon," said Kenofer. "No, don't look like that, it's months since he had the strength to walk into his own courtyard. He could have been carried to see the Choosing just now, but since he cannot walk he will not go. He prefers to lie in the shade of his room and wait."

"Wait for what?"

"For what the Mistress sends. And I understand him, for he is only twelve and yet I think he is dying, slowly wasting away. Had you not heard this at Myrtissos?"

Theano thought back to rumours that had come after Prince Geryon's infrequent visits to the Hill of the Kings. "We heard word of what seemed to be a fever, one that kept coming back, nothing more."

"Well, it is not talked about, not anywhere where word could be taken back to the queen. He is her only son, after all, and so far she refuses to believe the evidence of her own eyes. But Theano, I only told you this to warn you that this is a year not like the others since I came here as a boy. I first feared it months ago, before the priestess told me about my eyes and took all thoughts outside my own pain from my mind. Now, today, I have been shaken free of myself, to face what I already half knew."

He stopped again and lent his head against the wall in his characteristic gesture. Without opening his eyes he stretched out his hand.

"Give me the lyre."

She handed it to him and he settled it on his knee at the angle for playing. At first it was only single notes, seemingly with no pattern, then a downward phrase played several times, each a little different. Then his whole hand swept the strings, he crouched forward and there was a storm of rhythm and danger in the sound that flooded out. The sleepy servant stood up and came to the doorway to see what was happening. Kenofer did not look in his direction but he suddenly laid a hand across the strings and stilled them.

"Yes, I was right. Oh Kallisté, Kallisté, is it to come again?"

The pallor was back in his face and he was trembling. Theano was very frightened; the music had disturbed her deeply, the more so because she did not understand the meaning that it had for Kenofer. She had seen an old man at Myrtissos once, before the arrow of the Mistress had taken him, and he had slid down from his stool in the hall dying at their feet. Kenofer looked as that man had done. Was he going to die now, alone with her?

He had put down the lyre and his hands were fumbling with the folds of the blue robe over his knees. She took them in her own.

"Kenofer, are you ill, shall I take you home?" But had he the strength to walk as far as the House of Singing Birds and could she remember the way?

He still had not told her properly what was the matter. Kenofer drew his hands away and settled back against the wall, his eyes closed. He sat like that for a long while, then his head jerked forward a little way, as if he was dozing. He settled back more comfortably and slept again. Then he started to mutter under his breath.

Theano stood up and took a pace back. Kenofer did not wake. Still keeping her eyes on him, she walked across the courtyard to where the servant was still watching them.

"The Master is not well. See that he is not disturbed,"

she said, in what she hoped was the right tone of voice.

What had happened to Kenofer was beyond her own skill to aid, but somewhere in the maze of the palace there would be someone who could help. As she reached the corridor she knew who that was, Prince Geryon if she could only find him.

At the entrance to the main courtyard the guard turned to give her a quite different look from the one she had received when Kenofer was with her.

"Please," she said, and he saw the fear in her eyes and stopped grinning. "Could you tell me where to look for Prince Geryon?"

"He'll likely be in the Hall of the Summer Guard with the other fathers."

"Could . . . could I go there?" She was appalled at the thought.

"Are girls allowed? Yes, pretty ones like you, but usually not at this time of day. Still, it is the day of the Choosing and half the palace will be there. Do you know the way?"

She shook her head.

"Through the south entrance and follow the crowd."

The sun was directly overhead as she walked across the courtyard. It was so hot that the shade of the doorway on the far side was like the coolness of a cave. Two other girls, hand in hand, came in behind her; their skirts were saffron and lilac and they tinkled with bracelets, chattering like jays on a rooftop.

One flashed eyes made enormous by blue shadow under darkened brows.

"Who's this? We haven't seen you before! Going the same way as us, are you, dear? Now which of the Guard comes from your village?"

"My brother . . ." It wasn't true, but they had grown up together, and where Asterion was his father was likely to be.

"Oh, I see. Well, they all say that! Don't you know the way? We'll show you."

The girls put her between them and hustled her down the corridor. They were as hot as she was and the smell of their perfume was overpowering.

"That last one," giggled the taller girl. "Did you see his shoulders, he was perfect. Shall we try to make him laugh at the feast tonight? I love to see them blush!"

Theano suddenly began to have a real idea of what the banquet that night would be like. She had imagined something cheerful but decorous, like one of Prince Geryon's feasts. Of course the harvesters got drunk at the autumn festival but everyone expected that.

The girls dragged her up a flight of steps by their sticky little hands and through the doorway of a large hall. It was crowded but not so full of people that Theano could not see across it to the group who stood by a window on the far side; Asterion, another boy and three men. Prince Geryon had his back to her. The young men of the Guard were still in their finery, laughing too loudly at each other's jokes after the tension of the last hours. The room was high, painted with a freeze of bull-dancers and divided by two rows of pillars; doors led from it to the sleeping quarters. In the doorway Theano managed to pull away from her tormentors. There were not many other girls there, and hanging back she saw the length of the room as an impassable space. Then Asterion glanced casually towards the door.

She could see that he was tired, trying to listen politely to the conversation of men who were friends of his father, but weary now and wishing that the visitors would go and that he could bathe and be comfortable before the Guard began their duties at the banquet that night. There was so much to learn and the eyes that watched them would be curious and critical, remembering only too well the harvest of the summers that had gone before.

Asterion's eyes passed over her, settled on a girl in rose pink who was pirouetting on her toes in an imitation of one of the steps of the bull-dance and then jerked back. Theano took a step forward.

He touched his father's arm, murmured something and was then across the floor in a dozen strides, sweeping her out into the corridor with him.

"Theano! Now by the three mysteries of the Mistress, how did you get here? On the back of the sacred leopard?"

His face was in shadow, she could not tell if he was pleased or cross, and she had not time to find out.

"Kenofer brought me. I had to come because he needed me, and now he's ill."

"Here in the palace? Where?"

"In the courtyard outside Prince Laomedon's apartments."

"No! How is he ill?"

"It was during the Choosing, like marsh fever only worse. When I left him he was asleep and muttering. I didn't know what else to do."

"I would expect not!" He turned to go back into the hall, and then said over his shoulder. "You didn't sleep in the palace last night?"

"No, at the House of Singing Birds."

"And you've already had to find your way to the Hall of the Guard! Poor Theano. Wait, I'll tell my father."

He ran back across the hall, leaving Theano breathless with amazement at his approval.

She pressed back against the wall as a group of men came out. One ran an appraising eye over her and put out a hand; Prince Geryon was behind them. She slipped away from the enquiring hand and dropped a deep curtsy. The man coughed, muttered something she did not hear, and hurried to catch up his friends.

Prince Geryon seemed to take in the situation at a glance. "Come," he said. "This is no place to talk."

He led her quickly back down the stairs and out into the

colonnade around the courtyard, and Asterion followed them closely.

"Now, what happened?"

She told him quickly. "I thought he was going to die, and I was alone. Is he ill as well?" she asked.

"No, I don't think so. But I can guess what this is. There's no danger, at least not in the way you thought. But Kenofer would have wished for you to have been together for longer before the God came to him with such power. He's in the prince's courtyard, you said?"

The guard clicked to attention as Geryon strode past. In the entrance of the little court Theano hung back, suddenly afraid of what she would see although she had been gone such a short time. Then she felt that Asterion had taken her hand.

They stood together while Prince Geryon walked quietly across to where Kenofer lay on the bench. He was curled now with his face on his arm as if he were asleep on his bed at home, but at Geryon's footsteps his eyes opened slowly and he raised himself on an elbow, blinking. The prince went down on one knee and put out a hand to smooth back the long hair which had come loose from its clasp. It was a curiously gentle gesture from so big a man.

"Wake in peace," he said. "All's well, we're here."

"It was . . . there was the crowd and the drum beating. I thought . . . but I don't remember coming here."

"You were stronger than you knew, for Theano could not have carried you. But she came for the only help she knew, like a sensible child. The hand of the God was heavy on you, then?"

"Yes. I had been looking down on the dancing, seeing it as something bright but not lasting, like spring flowers—as it is now for me. Then it came; the power through me was so strong that I could neither breathe nor think. It was like the time of the earthshaking in Kallisté when I clung to a tree for safety while all that I knew fell apart around me. As if what I must soon leave will itself soon cease."

Asterion, still holding Theano's hand, felt the hair rise on the back of his neck. The girl beside him shivered, and he put an arm round her. Suddenly he was tired and the air in the small shaded courtyard felt chilly. What Kenofer was saying must be the dream of an artist's mind that could no longer contain itself. It was not possible that all this—the Summer Guard, the rituals of the palace, all Phaestos—could ever change.

Kenofer smiled into Geryon's concerned face. "Before I slept just now the beginning of a song for Phaestos came to me, but I will not play it now. Today is for Asterion and his song. I'm sorry I frightened you all. If what came to me was true the God will confirm it, if not then indeed my work here is done."

The prince stood up, still watching his friend dubiously, not sure that all had been told to him. "Whatever comes later, now you must rest and eat." He signed to the watching servant and gave him an order. "What time is it now? Two hours after noon. In four hours more you must be ready to play so that no one who hears you will ever forget it. Theano will stay with you, and I will come again."

Asterion felt himself dismissed. He released Theano and shook himself like a puppy who has been thrown into cold water and scrambled out. Was it all nothing then; truly? He must go back to the Hall of the Guard to prepare for the evening ahead, but even for him the colours of the day already seemed a little dimmer.

Kenofer sat in the great hall of the king and Theano stood behind him, as he himself had once stood behind the Master. The king and queen were late and the courtiers crowding between the pillars hummed like a hive about to swarm. It was just how Theano had imagined that morning that it would be; lamps blazed and flickered and the brilliant colours of painted walls and painted ladies glittering with gold and jewels hurt her eyes. Close by a woman with a shrill voice was laughing incessantly at the jokes of her companions.

Kenofer had been sitting with his head bowed, one hand resting lightly on the strings of the lyre. Now he straightened and turned to her, his mind drawing back from the thoughts that had held him silent during the hours of waiting, and smiled up at her with affection and care.

"I'm sorry that you must stand! It's only bards and great lords who may sit at banquets."

She bent down, her lips close to his ear. "I was thinking, this is the first time and now I won't come here again."

There was no time for him to answer her. A sudden hush spread down the hall so that the commands of the captain of the guard at the head of the royal staircase sounded loud. To the music of flutes and a little drum a procession was coming up from the king's room below: first the royal bodyguard, then dancers, almost naked and scattering rose petals, and behind them the king and queen themselves, erect, crowned with golden lilies, the painted faces as impassive as those of the griffons on the wall behind them but older than when Kenofer had first watched them enter their hall.

They turned to face their court and the people bowed like a flower-garden in a strong wind. The king and queen sat down, the chamberlain clapped his hands and beckoned, small tables were set beside their seats and the music began again.

But where were the Summer Guard? Theano had expected them to escort the king. Then she saw why they had not.

They were coming now, two by two up the staircase, carrying gifts to the king, Asterion again one of the leaders. The vases of bronze and stone and pottery had come from each part of the kingdom, the palace storerooms were already stuffed with precious things, but still more were always brought at the summer festival, at harvest and at midwinter and in spring.

The boys had rested and bathed; their shoulders shone with perfumed oil and their hair had been elaborately arranged in long curls and fringes. They walked barefoot across the painted floor of the palace and for this ceremony wore kilts that were thick with embroidery. Each pair in turn bowed to the royal couple and laid down their gifts. When all had done there was a word of command and the royal bodyguard came forward from their places round the throne and before each pillar. They put their spears into the hands of the Summer Guard, formed up in the centre of the hall for a final salute, and then marched away. Smoothly, as if following the steps of a dance, the new guard took their places, standing like figures of bronze.

There was a buzz of applause and approval, the music began again and the chamberlain signalled for the banquet to begin.

A table had been put beside Kenofer but he ate nothing, and the servant who brought him wine seemed to understand that it should be two parts water. The bard wetted his lips and set the cup down again. Theano was watching Asterion; he was on the far side where she could see him, very close to the king's throne, perhaps from respect for his father's blood. Geryon sat further off, quiet but watchful, studying the young solemn faces of the guard as if from them he would find the answer to the sending that had come that morning to Kenofer in the courtyard of the Choosing. The feasting continued, and then the time came when the last of the food was cleared away, and the king, his cup newly filled, signed to the chamberlain.

The chatter of voices faded and Kenofer raised his head and knew that his time had come. It was all so like it had been that first time, Geryon sat where he had sat then, only the Master was missing. Then he had been unprepared, now the music lay waiting in his quiet hands upon the lyre. It was the moment to play his song for the Chosen, yet he hesitated. He knew now, with a certainty that could only come from the God, that though he might still make music in the palaces of many kings he would never play again at Phaestos. Before the song for marching there was another that he must sing first.

Prince Geryon started as though a hand had been laid upon him and there was a quick hum of surprise that rustled down the hall like wind in barley as he struck the first notes. It was the song for Kallisté and as his clear true voice sang the words for the last time they were for Geryon alone. When he had finished there was a hum of polite appreciation, then the queen bent forward, the gilded lilies of her crown nodding.

"We had heard, bard, that you had made a new song for the day of the Choosing."

Kenofer rose and bowed, and then with a sudden change of mood swung round smiling to look from one expectant young face to another down the motionless rows of the Summer Guard.

"It is true. I have made a song of thunder for you who have come down from the mountain to shake us all. And as it is said that a well-made song will sing itself, let us see if I have laboured truly!"

He did not sit down again but rested his foot on the stool to support the lyre cradled in his left arm. His hand came down across the strings like a peel of thunder, then for the first time came the words of the chorus.

> *Though wind shake the forest*
> *The mountain is steadfast.*
> *White mountain, Mount Ida,*
> *Our strength is like yours.*
> *Though children fear thunder*
> *No more are we children,*
> *Together, together*
> *We march strong as men.*

137

Standing behind him Theano could not see Kenofer's face but she could watch Asterion. His eyes were blazing, all the uncertainty of the prince's court was gone, this was the crown, this was what he had dreamed of. In this moment, as Kenofer's voice continued with the words of the verse, he was completely happy, and when the chorus came again it was he who led the guard as they joined the bard in the music of their own song.

The thunder of young voices seemed to make the hot, crowded, brilliant hall tremble itself. Those around Kenofer moved forward so that he was almost lost in the crush. For one last time the chorus rang out, and then Theano realized that Kenofer was no longer singing. He was beside her, taking her arm and easing her back through the crowd and out through a side door into a buttery full of empty wine jugs and startled servants. In the cheering that followed the ending of the song he had not yet been missed.

"Come," he said, his own eyes now alight as Asterion's had been. "Now that is finished and we can go north."

14 ❧ The Horn of the Mistress

Asterion climbed the last dark steps and came out into a world of bright sky, strong wind blowing across the plain from the sea, and dusty plaster seamed with small cracks by the relentless beating of the sun. He was on the roof of the western part of the palace, high above the central courtyard; the sun was not far over the eastern horizon and the palace was waking slowly after a night of feasting; but lying on an unfamiliar pallet in the Hall of the Guard he had not been able to sleep beyond first light. After the nights spent in the open, high on the slopes of the mountain, the palace seemed hot and airless; besides, he was still young enough to want to explore.

The roof was an oblong block with a low parapet, edged on two sides by the moulded pairs of plaster horns which showed that the whole palace was consecrated to the Mistress. They made a spiky freeze, casting dark shadows across the dusty roof, and now that he saw them close, the red paint that covered them was flaking loose. Asterion went to the west side first and looked back along the ridge to the higher central summit topped by a guard post, and the roofs of the part of the town which was hidden by the curve of the hillside. Somewhere below Kenofer and Theano still slept. He would have liked to speak to them again, to thank the bard for the song which still hummed in his mind, but Kenofer was going north, it was not likely that they would meet again for a long while. And Theano—it was strange that he remembered her face so clearly, smiling across at him in the hall the night before. But today there would be no time for Theano either.

He walked back and looked down into the courtyard three stories below; the figures of the guards and servant-girls were small and bright as painted toys. Directly below him was the entrance to the palace shrine; above the noise of the wind he heard the sound of chanting. Asterion leaned far out, one hand on the curved red horn beside him that was nearly as tall as he.

A procession began to come out from the entrance of the shrine, first a priestess playing a double flute, then two others carrying a pottery offering-table. Suddenly a bird swooped low over the palace roof with a shrill cry; Asterion started, jerked back as he almost fell, and clutched at the horn to save himself. The plaster was old and patterned with small cracks; it broke away from the parapet, and as he threw himself clear it came loose in his hand and crashed down into the courtyard below.

There was a shrill screaming from several voices and then silence broken only by the sound of the wind. A man's voice below shouted an order. Asterion crouched, shaking so hard that his teeth chattered, gripping the broken base of the horn. He could not bear to look over to see what he had done, and yet he must. That weight of plaster falling from so high could have killed.

The guards, clattering up the staircase, found him on his knees staring down at the confusion below, the shattered offering-table, the cluster of priestesses trying to comfort a crying girl with blood on one arm and staining the flounces of her skirt. He had not tried to hide or to escape.

The captain, blinking in the strong sun after the darkness below, saw the red kilt of the Summer Guard, swore under his breath, and made the swift sign for the averting of bad luck with his hand.

Asterion heard them come out on to the roof and stood up slowly and stiffly, as if he had not moved for a long time. He put out a hand to the remaining horn to steady himself and then drew it back as if from something red-hot.

"It was like that, that was all. I touched it and it broke."

The captain looked up at a sky clear except for the circle of cloud that always gathered over Ida in the mornings. "May the Mistress lighten her hand upon Phaestos," he said.

Strymon had fastened the panniers containing Kenofer's robes on to the pack-donkey as it stood trying to nibble the young leaves in the courtyard of the House of Singing Birds. He went back to the small room that had been Kenofer's for so long now, as Theano was folding her palace dress into the top of the basket she had brought from Myrtissos. Today, for the beginning of the journey, she was wearing a plain linen shift like a servant.

She looked up smiling. "I'm ready." Actually she had hardly slept the night before and she felt tired and sick at the thought of what lay before her. The brief time of glory when she had seen Asterion named at the Choosing and had heard her brother sing his two greatest songs was over. She could not expect to see Asterion again for longer than she dared think of.

Theano followed Strymon down into the courtyard. Kenofer and the Master were sitting by the well, talking together quietly, although everything had been said, everything that could be put into words by two friends at such a parting as this.

Strymon looked up at the sun, already high in the sky. "You should have started at dawn," he said. "There's no shade on the road to the pass."

"We weren't ready," said Kenofer, smiling. "And we won't go far today."

But as he stood up there was the sound of hurrying feet outside in the lane and voices at the outer door.

It was Geryon who strode into the courtyard, but a Geryon they had never seen before, his face dark with emotion and his mouth set in a hard line.

Theano felt the sickening lurch in her stomach that comes before the certain telling of bad news. There was only one thing that could make the prince look like that. The name was on her lips even as Kenofer spoke it aloud.

"Asterion? What's happened?"

Geryon took his friend by the arms and then his hands dropped. Kenofer steadied him and pushed him down on to the rim of the well. The prince clenched his hands upon his knees and then looked up with pain-darkened eyes.

"He was too sure, he was always too sure. I don't think he understood that anything could touch him. And now it's come. A bird swooping from a clear sky."

"Prince Geryon, what has your son done?" asked the Master in his clear, precise voice.

"He has committed sacrilege, he has broken the table of offerings as it was being set out for the morning rites, and injured a priestess. He does not deny it, and yet although it was his hand that moved, his will was not behind it. It was as if another hand was over his." He told them what had happened that morning on the palace roof.

Kenofer had sat down beside him on the well rim with his hand on his friend's shoulder. As he listened, seeing in his mind a sharp, bright picture of Asterion and the swooping bird, another memory came, as insistent and overwhelming as sudden thunder. It was a picture of the same courtyard seen from below, the red horns dark shapes against the blazing blue of the noontide sky, the whirling dance of the Chosen, and the sending of the God. So it had been true and the confirmation had come.

He felt sick and powerless. What could men do when the gods turned away their faces? What comfort was there and what strength in his human arm about his friend's bent shoulders? Then he heard the words of his own song ringing inside his head.

Though children fear thunder
No more are we children.

He would do what he must and what he could. His own life already lay as broken about his feet again as it had been when he stood inside his shattered home on Kallisté; now the lives of Geryon and his son were broken too, but against their grief he was not quite powerless.

"Where is Asterion now?" he asked.

"The guards took him to the shrine of the Mistress in the valley. The priestess said that he should not be kept in the palace itself. The king is going there and the members of the council, those who can be reached in time. I came for you. It's come, hasn't it, what you saw yesterday?"

Kenofer stood up and strode across to the donkey. "My robe. If I'm going with you to the shrine of the Mistress I must go as the bard from Kallisté."

Theano went to him as he stood unbuckling the straps. "What will happen to him? Will they . . ." She could not put the thought that was tearing her into words.

"I don't know, it will be for the priestess to decide."

He pulled the robe over his head and as her hands came up automatically to straighten the folds he saw her face, streaked with tears; what she felt now and what lay deep in her heart for Asterion was too strong for concealment.

He bent to kiss her and to give her a small, steadying shake; then he turned back to Geryon.

"I'm ready. I think all may yet be well. The sign is clear now."

Theano watched them go and then turned to the Master instinctively, as if he were a kind grandfather she had known all her life. He stretched out a hand to her and she sank down on the ground by his knee. Strymon went to the donkey and unstrapped the panniers and then led him away; Theano heard him later inside the house talking to the pupils who had been waiting for their morning lesson, but no one came out into the courtyard. While the two by the well sat without speaking the house which had always echoed with music was also silent.

Geryon's chariot was waiting at the end of the lane. A small crowd had gathered, but they stood a little way off and watched the two men as they mounted in a strained silence, unlike any other crowd that Kenofer had seen in Phaestos. As Geryon turned the horses down the hill he saw the quick sign against evil made by half-concealed hands. The whole town was quiet, with few children playing in the streets and none of the usual groups of gossiping women. The omen was known, and it was as if the people were waiting for the palace, even the hill itself, to fall, even now, while they feared and murmured.

The two men did not speak as Geryon turned the team at the bottom of the hill and drove towards the great olive-grove of the Mistress in the plain below the palace. There were guards waiting at the entrance and one came forward to the horses' heads. The prince turned to Kenofer while they could still speak freely.

"What can we do?"

To see his friend baffled and in such pain almost shook the strange feeling of certainty that had been growing in Kenofer ever since he had left the House of Singing Birds. Geryon had said that Asterion was too sure, but it was from his father that he had inherited this confidence. Now for the first time in the years Kenofer had known him his friend was baffled. No matter, the feeling that was rising inside him now was as clear and as certain as the first springing of a new song. He did not know himself yet what he would do and say in the grove of the Mistress, but he knew that his own God would send the words as surely as the warning of this disaster had come to him the day before during the Choosing. It might be that this omen and his own were both the foreshadowings of something more terrible yet to come, but for the moment he could only act on the truth as he had seen it, and with it he could save his friends. For once the burden that the God had given him with his skill had come as a gift that he could take into his own hands and give to those he loved.

"Be calm, the God will give me the words." The prince did not understand, but something in Kenofer's face gave him the strength to walk into the grove beside the bard from Kalisté as calmly as if he had been a figure in a wall painting.

It was cool in the deep shade of the great trees, but in the centre there was an open place shimmering and golden in the strong morning sun, the dancing place of the Mistress. Today the grove was quiet and almost empty; no young priestesses would dance there while this omen hung over Phaestos. One of the older women met them and led them through the bright sunlight and into the darker shade beyond. Here the eldest priestess had her own small cell and there Asterion's fate would be decided. Kenofer looked at the straight back of the small elaborately-dressed woman who walked ahead of them and remembered his own mother dressed for her ceremonial duties. How would she have understood what had happened that morning on the palace roof? It was sure that a god had spoken, but what had been his will towards Asterion?

A small pillared portico led into a room that seemed completely dark after the light outside. Only as their eyes adjusted could they see it was already crowded; the King Inarchos, the queen and the old priestess were sitting on chairs against the far wall like statues of gods in a shrine, and there was the same heavy smell of perfumed oil and age. Asterion was standing by himself to one side. Kenofer moved out of the shaft of light that came in through the doorway and put his hand to his eyes; now when he needed to see clearly his vision was blurred.

Asterion had turned as they came in. His face was expressionless, pale and blank, as if he no longer knew what was happening to him, but at the sight of his father his eyes blazed back into life. Kenofer saw that he must have thought himself completely forsaken.

The oldest priestess was like a tiny shrivelled doll, almost lost in her bright wrappings; she put out a hand to silence the queen who had been speaking, and such was her authority that the queen stopped in mid-sentence.

"So. We have heard what was done and what was seen; of a sacrilege more terrible than any I remember, for it was not an offering dedicated to the Mistress that was destroyed, but the offering-table itself, the table that stands for our land. And yet this thing was done by one of our Chosen, newly dedicated to her, and not of his own will but as if a god took his hand and moved it."

The small flat voice ceased and Kenofer saw Asterion shiver.

"Can that hand draw back when the god moves it?" the bard asked. "Is not the hand that the god has taken sacred to him?"

There was a small murmur of sound from the men packed tight against the walls of the little stifling room, and a hiss from the queen, but the priestess made a cackle of sound that was almost a laugh.

"So, it is the bard from Kallisté. He of all of us should know what it is to feel the touch of a god. Tell us the signs, bard. Have I spoken truly?"

"Mother, you speak truly when you say that this act was not willed by Asterion. His Choosing and now this strange fate are only two threads, one light and one dark, in a great weaving whose pattern we cannot yet fully see. I understand now that I sang more truly than I knew when I gave to the Summer Guard a song of thunder. The God spoke to me, and with the force of thunder, even during the Choosing itself. I knew then that there was a doom upon their hope, but I did not see clearly enough to know that it would come through the deed of the son of my friend."

"Why should the gods speak to us of what they purpose; are we gods too? Tell me of the sending that came to you yesterday."

Then Kenofer, speaking as if to the priestess alone, told her what he had seen and felt the day before, feeling even as he spoke Asterion's hopeless gaze and the trust of Geryon. When he had finished he knew that it was not enough, he had not yet brought the priestess anything that would inspire her to act gently with Asterion, and her powers were absolute and could be very terrible.

"We were told that you had already left Phaestos," she said, after he had finished, and he thought that her mind had wandered, no strange thing in a woman of her age.

A guard in the doorway shifted and a shaft of brightness pierced the gloom and showed him her face more clearly. No, her eyes were sharp and shrewd, as if she were testing him.

"Mother, I should have gone an hour ago, I was already dressed for travel when the summons came, for I am going home. My own omens have shown me that I must go north, to Kallisté, to see the ruins of my own place while there is still light left in my eyes. Perhaps I shall be able to make an offering for my mother who also served the Mistress, if the ruins of her grove can still be found."

"You are going blind?"

Kenofer heard Geryon a little behind him draw in his breath. It was hard to hear it spoken aloud and so plainly.

"Yes. Much I have been given, I must not grudge what is to be taken."

"I have not heard if the grove of Kallisté is still deserted," said the priestess. "But I have heard that a voice of thunder still speaks from the island. Perhaps we should send our maker of omens with you to Kallisté. Perhaps there the Mistress will show more clearly what is her will for him and for Phaestos. Would you return then and bring her word to us?"

"Mother, that is a wise judgement," said the queen. "The boy cannot stay in Phaestos, but he is one of the Chosen after all. To harm him would bring an even greater doom upon us."

"You, Prince Geryon, take your son. He must be beyond the borders of Phaestos on the northern road by sunset. Do not think that you will see his face again unless he comes with a good word for the land from Kallisté."

Asterion dropped to his knees and bent to kiss the hem of the old woman's dress, but she twitched it away from him. Then Geryon raised his son and led him out into the sun and Kenofer followed them. Now that there was something practical to do the prince seemed to have come to life again.

"We shall need fast chariots. Wait here, I will go back to the palace to fetch what you will need, and Theano."

He ran to his chariot, taking the reins from the waiting guard and turned the horses in a scatter of small stones. The dust of his passing made a moving cloud between the orchards and up the steep road to the Hill of the Kings.

Kenofer took Asterion by the arm and led him some way past the grove and up a slope where they could wait above the road in the shade for his father's return. Below them the members of the council and the king and queen were leaving, but none of them looked back to where they stood. The priestess had spoken, Asterion had been banished and with him the danger of his sacrilege; now they would go home and try to pretend that it had never happened. But it was not over; the first danger had passed for Asterion himself, but the voice of the god had been in the breaking of the horn and the full understanding of his will was yet to be worked out.

Kenofer shook himself, and then started to take off his heavy singing robe; there was a long journey ahead. Asterion was gazing blankly at the dust cloud that still hung above the trees.

"Have you understood what is happening? You know that you must go with me to Kallisté? It was the only way that I could save you." Kenofer spoke clearly, as if the young man beside him was still a child.

When Asterion answered him Kenofer knew that he was indeed no longer the eager boy of the day before. Some part of him had been shattered as surely as the broken table of offerings. What he had feared for him on the hillside above Myrtissos five years before had come to the son of Geryon.

"No, I don't understand, how can I? But I know what I must do, where I must ride with you today. I don't know why, but Kenofer, you can see so many things, when to-morrow comes you must tell me again what I should do. I know that something has been taken from me today. I don't know how much is left. Perhaps the Mistress will show me on Kallisté."

But he was looking back at the white peak of Ida and the hills that hid Myrtissos and the high roofs of the palace as he spoke, and though the words were brave enough Kenofer saw the set white face break and crumple as a child's will when he has been punished. He longed to hug him as he could have hugged Theano, but Asterion was not ready for that yet, so he turned away and did not watch while the boy sat down on the ground as if his legs had given way under him and buried his face in his hands.

15 ❦ Grey Island

The first of the three chariots stopped below the slope where
Kenofer and Asterion waited. Geryon had driven fast down
from the palace hill and Theano had needed to hold on with
both hands; her hair was tied back under a scarf but already
there was grit between her teeth and the hot noontide sun
had given her the beginning of a headache. She was almost
afraid to look up at Asterion, coming down out of the trees
towards them. It was impossible that he should seem the same,
that he should be able to walk down and stand quietly at his
father's side after they had dismounted. If he had been crushed
himself by a falling horn and had been carried to the shrine
bleeding and unconscious then there would have been pity
for him in Phaestos. Broken limbs mend, but would the
wound Asterion had taken today ever heal?

There was no time for delay if they were to reach the border
high on the pass to Knossos by dusk. Geryon looked at the
two whom he loved, his son and his friend; they were both to
go from him in one day and what time would there be in the
short hours left to say to Asterion all that a father should say
to a son setting out on a journey from which he may not
return? There was no time for any of it now.

"You're ready, good. We've brought food, but we'll eat
when we're clear of the plain. Asterion, come with me."

Kenofer walked back to the second chariot, where one of
the prince's men stood ready, and Theano was waiting. She

looked small and tearstained and already bedraggled. He put his arms around her and held her tightly.

"Hush now, there's no more time for tears today. He's alive, though when Geryon came for me this morning I feared for him."

Theano sniffed and wiped her face on the end of her veil. "It's just . . . two days ago I was still at Myrtissos!"

"Two days? What will the next two bring us! Now, we must be quick, did you bring everything you need?"

"Yes, my basket and the panniers. Strymon put them in the third chariot, and food for the journey."

"My lyre!" Suddenly Kenofer felt almost sick. He had left the house so quickly that there had not even been time for that, and yet it was strange to be as long as an hour with it beyond the touch of his fingers.

"It's safe, the Master packed it himself." She ran to the third chariot and returned carrying the leather case in her arms.

"Are you ready?" The prince turned, the reins already in his hand.

The same captain who had driven her from home so short a time before was waiting to help her up into the third chariot. Theano found herself a place where she could stand among the bundles as the first chariot drew away. She did not look back at the high palace hill as they drove through the rich farmland of the plain, the corn long cut and the stubble baked hard and brittle. As they turned east below the foothills of Ida along the road that led to the pass there was fold after fold of olives growing down the slopes, giving some shade, with the fresh sharp green of vines growing wherever the olives could not get a foothold.

Even then she did not turn back. What had Phaestos brought her after the quiet years at Myrtissos but fear and the pain of watching those she loved in pain? The two triumphs of the day before were nothing now; they had been bought at too high a cost. There was something cold in the heart of the glittering splendour of the palace; did it only come from the ill-matched king and queen and their sickly child, or was the hand of the Mistress really heavy over the whole land? Holding tightly as the chariot jolted on the uneven road Theano had no time to think; only again through the pain there was for the second time the understanding that Asterion, to whom she had already said goodbye twice, was still with her. And now it might even be that at last she could do something to help him. More and more that thought calmed her as the hot and dusty hours passed.

They stopped once where there was good shade, to eat some of the food Strymon had prepared for them and drink water so warm from hours in a leather drinking bottle that it left Theano as thirsty as she had been before. Geryon and Kenofer went a little way off, where they could talk privately, and she sat alone, looking across at Asterion, wanting to speak to him. But he had thrown himself down in a patch of deep shade where there was still grass, and was lying on his front with his head buried in his arms. She understood that in all the hours since the bird swooped there had been no time when he was alone. There had been eyes upon him all the time, frightened, curious, implacable, seeking to read new omens into every word and every expression. No, she must not speak to him now.

Geryon did not give them long to rest. The sun was already climbing down the sky to the west over the sea, and the brightness was fading from the harsh colours of earth and trees. The distant water lay like a flat silver sheet, but higher a bank of mist had already hidden the foothills where Myrtissos lay. Geryon pushed on hard although the horses were labouring as they climbed higher; he had not missed the second cloud of dust on the lower bends of the road that showed that they were being followed at a discreet distance. There was no doubt that to the rulers of Phaestos, Asterion, who the day before had been so highly honoured, was now a danger and a threat of doom that must be carried beyond the borders of the land as a woman will carry some corrupted thing far from her house door.

The frontier post lay near a village already high in the foothills. Geryon drew up a little way below, just as the sun sank for the last time into a bank of cloud and the upper slopes of the mountains that had still been pink and gold went grey. The two guards who had driven the other chariots tethered their horses and went up into the village in search of a donkey to carry the baggage. Geryon and the three who were to journey further were left alone together, but their leavetaking would need to be swift if the prince was to get even part of the way home before darkness made the road unsafe.

He turned first to Theano, and as he smiled at her there was the ghost of the old familiar warmth in his eyes.

"Goodbye, adopted daughter of Myrtissos. So now you must care for two men, not one, and I am certain, sensible as you are, that you will do it well."

She gave him the curtsy that would have looked better in her usual long flounced skirt, but he laughed suddenly, and bent down and hugged her. He was so big a man that she felt as if a bull had fallen on her.

Then he turned to the other two. It might be that in one month or three or four they would return and yet Theano understood as she watched them that none of the three dared hope for so much. This must be a farewell that would stand for a final parting to be carried in the heart for a lifetime, if need be.

Kenofer said, "Oh my friend!" and the two men kissed, but gently, not as the prince had kissed Theano.

Geryon said only the name, "Kenofer." But in the look that went with it there was more than a farewell, that reading of a face that tries to make a memory that will not fade. There was also some message that she could not understand and that needed no words. Then the prince turned to his son.

"There is no man with whom I would sooner see you set out on this journey than Kenofer, and perhaps out of this evil day there is one small crumb of comfort to be found. These two would have travelled from Phaestos alone, a girl who has only once before left her home, and Kenofer who bears the burden of his dimming eyes. You have been sent to Kallisté to find your own fate, but I know that you can also make the way easier for my friends."

Asterion drew himself up almost as if he were a young soldier receiving orders from his officer. For the first time he looked across at Theano, as if he had hardly been aware before that she was there. At something he saw his own face changed, and as the girl and the young man looked at each other the eyes of the older men met too.

Then the guards brought a donkey down from the village and began to load the panniers and a bundle that Geryon had brought for his own son.

"I've spoken for beds for you for the night with the head-man," said the older of the guards. "We've come swiftly and no word of what happened has reached so far. It would be better to say nothing of the reason for your journey."

Asterion was still wearing the kilt of a member of the Summer Guard. His father rummaged in the bundle.

"Put this on quickly. Anyone who sees you dressed like that will know that something is wrong."

His face blank again with the look of incomprehension that it had worn all day, Asterion unbuckled the broad belt that held his kilt over a padded loincloth and put on another plainer one that he had worn at home. Then he stood, still holding the red, gaily embroidered linen, its colour already drained from it by the fading light, as if he was only now understanding that after one day he would never wear it again. Geryon took it from him quickly and tossed it into the chariot. He put up a hand to touch his son's long hair, braided in tresses from a high knot on the crown of the head.

"Theano must see to that for you tomorrow. You will need it shorter for travel."

The two guards had already mounted their chariots and driven a little way down the road. It was time. The prince took his son by the shoulders, kissed him once and said, "May the hand of the Mistress preserve you," and then turned and mounted. His hands already on the reins, he looked down at them for one long moment more, Kenofer standing with his arm round Theano, Asterion a little apart. Then he drove off into the dusk without looking back.

Kenofer waited until the chariot was round the turn of the road and then gave Theano a little push.

"Now we must be quick. We shall not get much of a welcome if we come in out of the darkness like robbers." Then to Asterion he said quietly, "It is the first hour, the time when one cry would bring him back, that is the worst. Believe me, it can only grow easier."

"Kenofer, I hope you're right."

Asterion had not spoken for so long that his voice was husky and unlike itself, but he turned, suffering Kenofer's hand to stay upon his shoulder as they began to walk up the steep slope to the village. In the sudden darkness Kenofer found himself walking blind; his eyes were tired and strained from the glare and dazzle of the afternoon and he could see nothing. When he stumbled his hand on Asterion's shoulder saved him. The boy started, and then took his arm.

"I'm sorry, I should have known. Let me help you."

It was more than Kenofer needed, but he was glad that they should be walking together even so when, almost without knowing it, the moment came when they crossed the borders of Phaestos.

The first part of their journey took them four days, and by the time they had reached the lands of the High King they were all dusty and brown enough to be unremarkable among the many travellers along the royal road to the House of the

Double Axe. Theano had cut Asterion's hair shoulder-length on the first morning. Kenofer had warned them that it might not be safe to stop there; he himself was too well known and the High King might try to delay him, and by now the omen of the falling horn must be known even as far as the north coast. Kenofer had become increasingly silent as the hot days among the high sunbaked ridges had passed. Not once had he opened the case and laid his hands on the strings of his lyre. It was as if he were already hearing the distant call of a music they could not hear. He walked ahead leading the donkey—he was better with her than Asterion after his years of wandering— setting a pace that Theano could keep up with, but too withdrawn from his younger companions to be drawn into casual chatter.

By the time they had reached Knossos and her face was brown, Theano had become accustomed to the rhythm of the journey; after all, they had done the same thing for four days running, and nothing more alarming had happened than the occasional brush with shepherds' dogs who had been driven off by well-aimed stones from Asterion. From the moment that the chariots had left them on the first night Asterion had never once mentioned Phaestos as they walked together. He had the air of someone who has received a disfiguring wound but who can manage his life quite well so long as no one speaks of it.

He asked Theano many questions about Kalliste, and although it was difficult at first because she had tried to forget her old home, for Asterion she was willing to remember. As they walked together talking like brother and sister the shyness between them faded.

They came in the end to a place where the royal road led past the palace, and there they stopped as all the travellers ahead of them had. Theano had seen the palace of Phaestos and had expected no more of the House of the Axe, but when it lay before her across a narrow ravine, terrace above columned terrace, courtyards and halls and storerooms all crowded together across the summit of the hill opposite above the lower houses of the town, she knew that what she had already seen had been like a head-man's hut by comparison. She was glad then that they were to pass it by, for she had seen enough of palaces.

Even as they stood gazing they heard what seemed like thunder. It was a little before noon, and the sky was overcast, but a wind was blowing from the north. Kenofer led them on past the palace and it was late afternoon when they reached Amnissos, where they hoped to find a boat to take them north. The wind off the sea blew grit and dust across the market-place above the beach and had drawn light cloud across the sun. North lay the grey shape of Dia, the small island which gave shelter to the harbour; in the strait between the sea was calm, but further down the coast waves rolled in, flecked with foam.

After he had disposed of the donkey Kenofer found the others somewhere to shelter from the wind in the doorway of a sailmakers' shed and then went down towards the drinking places full of sailors kept in port by the contrary wind. Asterion, grim-faced, his long cloak tugged by the wind, stood between Theano and the stares of passers-by. Kenofer was gone a long time.

Asterion glanced over his shoulder at the beach. A tub-shaped merchantman had been pulled up high and lay over on one side like a spilled basket, there were a few fishing-boats and one of the High King's scout-boats, nothing more.

"He'll never find a boat," he said. "Even if the wind wasn't dead against us there's nothing here to make the crossing to Kallisté."

"If we must he'll find something," said Theano. "Remember he believes that his God is calling him."

"Don't say that, not now!" Asterion glanced northwards again. Already Kallisté was so close, and he had caught something of Theano's fear of the place.

He looked down at her and saw that she was exhausted. Her brown hair was thick with dust and her bare feet below the ragged hem of her dress were dirty. But she had not complained; all this was no more than a man, and one of the guard of Phaestos, should be expected to bear. Theano, the quiet one back at Myrtissos, was proving as enduring as any man.

But he must not think of Myrtissos; if he remembered his home and his father he would turn and run back across the mountains to the south.

Out to sea there was a flash of sheet lightning and the distant sound of thunder. A fisherman passing with a basket on his hip paused and looked north.

"There it is again. Summer lightning or the island? The fish must know something even if we don't."

"Are you going out tonight?" asked Asterion.

The man spat in the dust. "Why waste the sweat? The fish won't come till the wind changes."

Kenofer, coming up unexpectedly between the sheds behind them, heard the last of that. "It'll change tonight. You should see that your nets are ready."

The man gave him a startled look and hurried off. Asterion stared after him and then turned back to Kenofer, who was standing looking out to sea in the fading light, shading his eyes with his hand.

"How can you be so sure?"

"Can't you feel?"

A handful of the short broken fronds of seaweed that littered the beach blew across the dusty ground and then fell, as the breeze dropped and Asterion's cloak hung still.

"The wind's dropping and the sea will go down tonight, and we shall sail at dawn."

"You've found a boat?" asked Theano.

Kenofer looked at her as if amazed at the question. "Of course."

158

They picked up the bundles and trailed after him into the gathering darkness. Far along the beach, beyond the last of the fishermen's huts, was the largest of the boats. In the lee of her hull a small fire burnt, the bleached wood from above the storm mark spurting blue and green with dried salt. The men lying around it moved over to give them room with no comment, except for one, the tallest, a fat man with a crooked nose and only the remains of a fringe of grey hair round the high dome of his head, burnished by the sun.

"Sing us a song, bard. It will pay for your supper and that of the pretty lady. The boy can work for his tomorrow."

"I'll eat first, Kleobis, and then sing. Have you anything that won't harm my gentle stomach?" Kenofer smiled at the big sailor, who had carried him across the sea before.

He had not sung since the last night at Phaestos. Theano lay wrapped in her cloak looking at the dark sky above the hull of the boat, listening to him. Kenofer was singing softly. If word spread down the beach who he was half the town would come to listen. The sky had cleared with the dusk and there were a few faint stars. Far off the thunder still sounded from time to time over the sea. Then one sound came louder than the others, and a shiver as if she lay already in the boat at sea and not on dry land. It was a small earthshaking.

Kenofer stopped in mid-phrase. Kleobis said, "Again! Your God is impatient, bard. I don't know why I listened to you this afternoon, but I won't go back on a bargain. Get some sleep now, tomorrow night won't be so good."

And the night after that they were far away in a boat that creaked and complained, running north under sail in a hot wind from the south, as Kenofer had promised. Out beyond Dia they had met the swell from the night before, but Kleobis had not slackened sail. As the passengers huddled together in what shelter there was, clear of the bare feet of the sailors and Kleobis's appalling oaths when a wave-crest, chopped off short, slapped over the side and caught him on the mouth,

Theano wondered if they would all die out there. They were far out of sight of the Great Island now; she had been sick and so had Asterion, but Kenofer sat in a daze, watching the hurrying lines of waves.

As the day had drawn on, her stomach settled and so had the sea. Even the memory of Phaestos falling far to the south of them was fading. During the first night they had huddled together for warmth and Theano had lain close to Asterion. If she had known they would have been like this five days ago, before the Choosing, she would have thought it a dream more impossible than anything that had happened to her during the difficult days between. Then she had worshipped a boy she had not really known; now they had been tired and frightened together, she had seen him blazing with joy, and silent under the weight of bitter disappointment and sorrow. The Mistress had already given her much more of him than she had imagined would ever be hers. Back at Myrtissos she had thought of him only as someone handsome and gay; the Asterion she now knew was brave as well, and had not complained over either the discomforts of the journey or the deeper pain within his heart. She would not look beyond the coming days, whatever they might hold. She would not snatch at the Mistress's gift.

The thunder from the north came again. She heard him sigh and raise himself on one elbow so that he could see better, and his head made a dark shape against the paler sky. Kenofer, wrapped in his cloak, stood beside Kleobis where the big man swayed, the weight of his body instinctively controlling the steering oar.

"Does he hear it?" whispered Asterion. "The sailors call it the voice of Kallisté. They say that the island has been thundering for months, and that it flashes fire at night, and white dust lies everywhere. Theano, what is Kenofer taking us to? Are there still people alive there? Will the Mistress be able to give me the word I need?"

"Isander the architect went north two months ago. There

were people living there who had sent for him to have his advice about rebuilding. The thundering can't have been so bad then. Perhaps the sailors are only trying to frighten us."

"But we can hear. Kenofer can hear. Is there some sacrifice that he needs to make on Kallisté whatever the cost? Or Theano, are we the sacrifice? Shall we ever leave Kallisté?"

"No!"

She had spoken louder than she meant, but the sailors lying close to them had not stirred. The very thought made her sick. Kenofer might see some fate like that for himself; she no longer understood what power it was that drove him onwards. But he would never have taken her from Myrtissos for a journey with no hope of a good end.

She felt Asterion move again. Theano had not known how much she was trembling until he put his arm around her.

"Theano, I'm sorry. I didn't mean it, I owe him so much and I trust him. I suppose it's just that there is a pattern that his God shows him a little at a time and we never see. And . . . we're so close. You lie here as calmly as if you were at home. And I'm frightened, and no . . . I can't even be sick, there's nothing more to come!"

He gave a little laugh then that she felt rather than heard, as he held her in a way that comforted them both. "Go back to sleep, you're far more sensible than I am."

The second day passed like the first, in a dream of wind and spray and constant motion. Salt dried on their skins and reddened their eyes, and their clothes were never dry. Theano tried not to think of the fresh springs of Myrtissos as Kleobis passed round brackish water in a leather bottle; she dreamed of water the second night, and woke to feel the cool drops of a shower pass over the boat and fall on her upturned face. When she woke for the second time the sky was light, the sailors were all awake and the boat had tilted as if they were all peering one way. Even the movement was different; they were running through calm water.

Theano sat up, shook the tangled hair out of her eyes, wrapped her cloak around her and stood up. Kallisté had come up during the night and now hung high above them, grey and ghostlike in the dawn light. It filled the whole horizon to the north, while to the west and east capes on either side of the shallow harbour ran out to make the sheltered bay they had now entered. High up, so that she had to bend far back to see, the peaks inland seemed tangled in low cloud.

Straight ahead was a broken hilly place down by the shore; that was where the town should have been. But it was still and dark, like a dwelling place for the dead. Surely Isander could not be there, surely no one could live on that grey island. Kenofer had been standing with the men in the prow. He saw that she was awake and came back to her. His eyes were red-rimmed from lack of sleep, but they glittered in a new way as the light strengthened and the first colour came into the eastern sky.

"There she is, Kallisté the beautiful one. And we thought we would never see her again."

He put an arm around her to hold her steady. "Why did you never come back before?" she asked.

"Before there would have been only ghosts to play to. Now tell me, what can you see? The Governor's house was to the east, but it was burnt, I remember."

"Kenofer, I thought everything was grey because it was so early, but it isn't. It's as if there's dust everywhere, nothing has any colour. Where the orchards were, up behind the town, there are only the stumps of trees left, everything's dead."

They were much closer in now. A horrified murmuring had come from the men in the prow as they too saw what Theano had seen; then everyone fell silent. Looking again at the broken peaks of the central mountain, Theano saw that it was not cloud upon them but smoke.

"Look, on the shore." Asterion was shouting and pointing. A man was running, stumbling in banks of shingle. They were close enough to see the ruins of the breakwater and the lower parts of the town. The man had disappeared between the broken walls. As they grated in up the beach he came out followed by five others, dusty, hollow-eyed men with half-grown beards.

"If that's Isander, what's come to the boat that brought him?" said Kleobis, as his own men splashed across the side to drag them clear of the water.

The sun came over the eastern headland, touched the boat with gold and showed them the haggard face of the chief architect of Phaestos, as he stood knee-deep in the water, struck silent with amazement at the sight of Kenofer.

As the boat finally grounded, it tipped alarmingly, throwing Theano into a heap in the bottom; by the time she had picked herself up she was the last person on board. She did not see Kenofer's face as he jumped down and waded through the shifting pebbles to the land. Only Asterion turned back for her and caught her as she jumped over the side, so they came together to Kallisté, the island of dust and ghosts; she returning to the shore she had left as a child in such fear, and Asterion seeing at last the still eye of the storm raised by a God, the place from which a God still spoke through the hands of Kenofer.

16 ⚵ The Rock

They huddled together close to the water's edge, in the shelter of the ruined breakwater. The sun was up, but the whole south side of the island was shadowed by the smoke that came from the peaks. The rumbling that had seemed like thunder was all around them and shaking the ground beneath their feet. As the gusting wind, shifting again towards the north and east, blew the plume of smoke down low over the ruined town, the fine dust which already powdered everything was still falling, lying in the folds of their clothes and the creases round their eyes, and gritting between their teeth. And with the smoke came wafts of an acrid smell which caught in the throat and made them cough.

"We've been here more than a month," said Isander. "We had been told that the first settlers came back last autumn and there was hope that rebuilding could really begin. That's why I was sent for."

"But you came too late," said Kenofer.

"Yes, the mountain was already thundering when we left Amnissos, but we thought it was no more than a summer storm. When we arrived we could not believe our eyes, but we landed all the same."

"And was no one here?" asked Asterion.

"No one alive, but the wind was set fair for Melos, they must have gone that way. There's nothing left, Kenofer. We found the remains of the huts they had built and the partly cleared streets, but already they were silting up with ash and behind the town there's nothing. Nothing can grow in this ash, and the foul vapours that come down from the mountain."

"And the shrine of the Mistress?" Theano saw that Asterion's hands were clenched tightly together on his knees.

"I don't know, we could not get so far. On the second morning we were here the whole island shook, there was fire from the mountain and rocks came down smoking and blazing. There is no way back up the valley behind the town. The road has gone, the cliffs are down, and the trees of the Mistress's grove must be charred and broken. There have been no offerings made there since the first great earthshaking."

Asterion bowed his head; Theano, sitting beside him, dared to slip her hand into his and he took it.

"What happened to your boat?" asked Kleobis.

"One of the falling rocks stove in the bottom and sank it. It was as if the God himself was throwing them."

"So Kallisté called you just as she has called to others," said Kenofer.

"Yes, Kallisté . . . to see it just once more! You understand, or why are you here? Not to save us, you could not have known that we were in danger." In his exhaustion it had not occurred to him to question the presence of Asterion.

Kenofer did not answer his question. He had taken his lyre from its bag, seemingly to see if it had suffered in the sea crossing, and now his strong fingers tested the strings. A thin film of dust settled on the polished wood. He bent his head and played one phrase from the lament for Kallisté.

"Yes," said Isander. "You understand."

"And now what have we found? Ashes and death. Where does your God lead us now, Kenofer?" asked Asterion.

"And where must we follow?" Theano thought in her heart.

Kleobis, standing a little way back from the group, turned towards them. "The wind's coming round, it's fair for Melos again and I like the feel of this place less than a hurricane with my mast gone. We'll be heavy laden and need an easy crossing. Are you coming?"

"You'll want to refill the water-skins, if any wells are still open. Just one hour, Kleobis."

"One hour and I shall sail. With or without you."

He shouted to his men to be quick with the skins, while Isander went to show them where they had found water.

"What will you do with your hour, Kenofer?" asked Asterion.

"Come and see."

He led them towards where the main street of the town had been. Five years before he had climbed it with Phormio when they had come down from the Governor's palace. Now it was choked with walls that had fallen outwards into it in the great earthshaking, and the ruin and dirt of years. Although his eyes were weak and it had all changed he seemed to know by instinct which way to take; to Theano it was completely unfamiliar.

"Will you carry this?" He gave his lyre to Asterion, and then led them upwards over the piles of mudbrick rubble and stone foundations.

It was some way before he found the place he wanted, high above the harbour, and Theano was already beginning to look back longingly towards the tiny figures on the shore. She knew where they were going now and did not want to see it, and she was terrified that Kleobis would leave them behind. Then Kenofer stopped.

"It was here."

Part of the outer wall still stood, but the courtyard was choked with rubbish and the trunk of some shrub growing from the ruins stuck out of the mess of broken plaster, but stripped of its leaves by the recent fall of ash. One of the doorposts was still in place. Kenofer went down on his knees just inside and peered shortsightedly at the rubbish. Theano bent down beside him and pulled at a piece of wood that stuck out; it came with a shower of the fragments that had come from the walls of one of the upper rooms. She caught her breath at what she saw and burrowed further.

"Oh look!"

She held in her hands a piece of plaster no larger than her palm, but on it, the bright colours protected over the years by the rubbish higher up, was the perfect painted head of a swallow, its eye still sharp and keen.

Kenofer took it from her. "Father painted that, it was on the wall of Mother's room."

He stood up then and reached out his hand for the lyre. Asterion gave it to him and then drew Theano back through the broken doorway, and they stood there, his arm around her while she held the piece of painted plaster. Then the greatest bard ever to come from the island played there for the last time.

It was the lament for the orchards of Kalliste, and Kenofer had never played it better, not even that first time in the king's hall of Phaestos when it had brought him the friendship of Prince Geryon.

There were no birds now left on Kalliste, and when he had finished there was no sound except from the wind, blowing small pebbles along the top of a broken wall. Even the rumbling from the mountain had stopped. Then a shout, very faint against the wind, came from far below, and Kenofer turned and walked out through the doorway of his father's house for the last time.

Huddled close with hardly room to sit, no one spoke in the boat until they were well clear of the western headland and out in the open sea, heading towards Melos. Then Asterion asked Kleobis how long the crossing would take.

"If this wind holds, we could make landfall tomorrow some time. Should be before dusk. It'll be an uncomfortable night."

"But better than Kalliste," said Isander.

They all looked back then, except Kenofer, whose red-rimmed eyes were closed. The peaks of the mountain were clear this far out, a jagged cone beneath its plume of smoke. As they watched it seemed that lightning flashed and there was a red glow on the base of the cloud, and the thunder of the God spoke again.

Kleobis made the sign against ill luck and set his course nearer the freshening wind. It was towards midday of the next day that they were south of Melos, but by then the wind had backed part way to the north and had blown them south during the night. The bare south coast of the island lay across the horizon, but there was no hope, with the boat so heavily laden, of beating in towards the harbour of Philakopi. Kleobis could only run west with the wind in his sails.

When he saw that they could not make the harbour, Kenofer stood up and picked his way carefully across the sprawling legs of the seasick passengers to stand again at Kleobis's side. Now Kallisté was at last far behind and below the horizon he seemed almost gay.

"Where will the God send us now?"

"Which God? I only know one, the sailors' God beneath the sea, and I don't think we have his favour. At this rate we shall be blown straight to Achaea, and may the north men take us in!"

He would say no more. Darkness fell and there was no sound in the boat above the creaking of wood and wind and water except for the youngest of Isander's companions, who was still miserably sick and crying in a half-waking doze. Towards midnight when Theano woke, not for the first time, she felt that Kenofer lying beside her was also awake. He heard the change in her breathing and turned towards her.

"Theano, we did not dream of this when we first talked in the sun at Myrtissos. And you wouldn't have come with me then if you had known, nor would I have asked you."

"I don't know." It was hard to think back to what seemed

so long ago and far behind her. Myrtissos seemed farther away than the winters of her childhood. And then she knew for sure, and she felt for his hand in the dark so that he would know she spoke the truth even though he could not see her face.

"No, I would still have come. Aethra was the daring one, but I think she would have hated this even more than I do. It's cold, and I'm hungry and sick at the same time, but you are here, we two who are left, and Asterion. Kenofer, what's Achaea like?"

It was a little time before he could speak, and when he did he kept his voice down, as if he were talking of ordinary things.

"It is a great land, some of the people of Kallisté came from there. The mountains and valleys are like the Great Island, but it's larger and the people live less close. It goes on to the north further than anyone I have known has ever travelled."

"Will the people there think of us as kinfolk?" asked Theano.

"If our God is good."

He lay thinking back in the darkness over the last days, the time since he had walked in the early morning to Myrtissos. How long ago was it now? Nine days, and in that time the God had changed the direction of his life again and again, as if he were a dry leaf caught and dropped and twisted in the autumn winds. Yet although the path had been strange the will of his God in it had seemed to grow stronger all the time. He had been sure that he must come to Kallisté, and yet now that he had obeyed that command there had been nothing there. He was adrift on a dark sea and could no longer control the way ahead for himself or for Theano and Asterion. Yet when the time came to strike free from the strong current that now carried them he was certain that he would know.

But he fell asleep thinking of the long cruel coast with its sheer rocks and few good landings that faced east towards Melos and the islands.

They were in sight of land again by midday on the next day,

north and south along the horizon as far as they could see. As the sun passed overhead towards the distant peaks they grew flat and grey, sharp-edged as a painter might draw them, the shape of the foothills lost in shadow. Then Kleobis gave a great roar and put over the steering oar so that they swung towards a high crest of mountains further south.

"Minoa! A good landfall for any boat out of Amnissos. We shall eat among friends tonight."

Soon they could all see what he had seen, a great rock jutting out like a table from the flatter coastline between the sea and the mountains. A great table, almost sheer-sided, joined to the land by an isthmus, and on that a town, and the masts of beached ships, and the smoke of fires. They watched in silence as Kleobis brought the boat further round parallel with the coast, and marvelled at the height of the cliffs of the great rock. At the western end a light pricked out, clear against a sky washed gold and green, as the sun dipped behind the western mountains.

Theano pointed. "What's that?" But Kenofer could not see.

"The guard post. The High King has a trading station here. It's his best harbour on all the south-eastern shores of Achaea," said Kleobis. Then he yelled to his men to reef the sail.

They had been seen from the shore and men were running to help pull them in, splashing through the shallow waves. After the grey bleakness of Kallisté Theano found herself close to tears. She was carried safe to shore in the arms of a sailor and set down on the strange beach, and then they were taken to the house of the commander of the trading post. After they had been washed and fed and put to sleep under clean covers in a room with walls and a floor that stayed still, Theano was too tired to sleep easily or deeply. Now more than ever when they were safe from the sea, Kallisté towered in her dreams and she could see the red glow of fires and hear the thunder.

When she woke in the half light before dawn, a mainland cock crowed as she reached for the bed-cover which had slipped, and the thunder was still there. She could see that Kenofer was also awake, sitting up and listening.

"Do you hear it too? It can't be Kallisté, not here."

He got out of bed and felt his way over to her. "I've been listening a long time. Theano, we must get up, can you find your clothes?"

"What is it?"

"I don't know, but I feel . . ." She put up a hand to touch him and he was shaking as if with fever, as he had on the morning of the Choosing. She knew then what had come to him.

"What must we do?"

"I don't know, but as something seemed to draw me northward, now I know we must go higher up."

"Into the mountains?"

"No, there isn't time."

"To the rock?"

Kenofer let out his breath in a gasp that sounded like relief. "Yes, the rock. And today my eyes are dim, Theano. I can see within my mind, but you must guide my steps. We will climb the rock together."

17 ❀ The Pillar of Night

Below the guard post at the western end of the rock Kenofer stood with his arm around Theano. Asterion was higher up behind them, shouting up to the guard. Further down in a hollow sheltered from the wind were Isander and the men who had come with him. The whole top of the rock was a garden of purple vetch and pink rock roses, thyme and oleander. A path led between outcrops of stone from the eastern end where the high table shelved down towards the south and a way zigzagged up from the isthmus.

Theano had packed a basket of food and Asterion had carried a water-jar for them. To the people of Minoa it must have looked like a picnic, except that the captain's wife had been puzzled that they wanted to start so early. None of them knew why they had come, not even Kenofer, but by now the others did not doubt that he must be obeyed when the look they saw there now was in his fading eyes. This morning he seemed no longer the young man he still was in years; the gift of the God pressed heavily upon him.

Far to the east the blue sea grew misty before it joined the sky, so that there was no horizon, but from that direction the thunder still sounded, louder or softer as the wind came in gusts so high up.

Kenofer let his breath go in a long sigh. "Now we can sleep."

There was a sheltered place beneath the walls of the guard post, out of both sun and wind. Theano spread their cloaks there and lay down beside her brother. The night had been restless and the exhaustion of their journey was still upon them; it would be good to sleep, safe from both Kallisté and the troubles of the Great Island.

It was long after noon when she woke. Asterion was crouching beside her, and although the sun had passed overhead the sky was now overcast and it seemed unexpectedly quiet.

Then she saw his face. "What is it?"

"I don't know. I didn't sleep long and I've been watching the sky for a long time. Look."

He pulled her to her feet and pointed eastward. What seemed to be a great bank of cloud lay across the horizon, it was the skirts of that which were between them and the sun.

"It's quiet," she said.

"I know. Now it is. The thunder was worse just now, I thought it would wake you. Now it's stopped."

"No!"

The roar that came shook the rock beneath their feet. The guard on the wall above shouted and pointed, and Kenofer cried out as he woke. The cloud on the horizon billowed and surged upwards, breaking into a great pillar of darkness that mounted higher and higher like a colossal water-spout. And all the time the roaring continued. The wind was strong now; the pillar of cloud blossomed into a great tree, the branches wavering and spreading southwards.

Still clinging together, they crouched down in what shelter they could find. The guards were signalling down to the people at the harbour below, and tiny figures began to stream across the isthmus. Slowly time passed. The great tree of cloud had blown away and there was only a wall of darkness across the sea which crept slowly closer towards them. The thunder continued, unceasing, stunning them and making thought impossible. Then the sun sank behind them in a livid orange glow and the air became full of the fine dust they had felt before on Kallisté.

Kenofer had not moved for hours. Most of the people of the little town were clustered lower down the sloping table of rock, and Kleobis and his sailors were with them. Several small fires glowed, and the guard at the post was changed. They had not eaten all day and now Theano opened the basket, shaking dust from the wrappings, and gave them bread, but it stuck in their dry mouths, and to each of them it seemed that they should be sparing with the water. Theano wrapped the broken remains of the bread away and spread a cloak beneath the rocks.

"Come."

As if Kenofer were old and already blind she led him to it, settled him for the night and lay down again beside him. She heard Isander and his friends lie down nearby for what little comfort they could each gain from their closeness together. Asterion still sat wrapped in his cloak, staring out to sea.

"The God will wake us if he wills," Theano said softly. "Asterion, come and rest now."

He lay down beside her in his cloak, understanding her thought that they did not know what calls on their strength their fate on the morrow would bring. He wondered again at her calmness as she cared for her brother and made herself busy about the small and necessary tasks that he had hardly noticed before that women did. Theano was strong, even though she might not realise it herself.

All night the dust fell, and the thunder came and went upon the wind, too loud for them to sleep. They lay awake, feeling the rock beneath them shake, taking what rest they could; at last, stiff and cold, with the pebbles and sharp stalks of thyme hard and bruising beneath his cloak, Asterion felt a change in the air. The wind that had blown strongly all night had dropped and even the thunder was less. Then the air moved again with the different feel of the dawn wind. But would the sun ever rise above the great darkness to the east?

Something came in the end, not morning, but a greyness

with a smear of pink below it. Asterion propped himself against the rocks and waited. Glancing down he saw that Theano's eyes were open, but Kenofer was lying with his arm across her and she could not move without disturbing him.

The light spread, first green then lemon overhead so that the outlines of the rock became clear, and then orange low down over the sea with the bank of darkness between. He stood up and climbed a few paces higher to see better. It was so quiet that he wondered, with a hope that came more from desperation than belief, if the worst was over and Kallisté had achieved her fate. Then when he was about to turn back to wake Kenofer it came.

A flash brighter than the sun engulfed the sky, he stumbled back, hands to his eyes, and fell on the rough rock. The blackness lasted only a moment and then the great fire blazed red through the skin of his hands a second time and with it in the darkness that followed a roar of sound that seemed to take him and roll him over as helpless as a swimmer caught by a giant wave. And what seemed like a wave caught him too, a great blast of air that raced across the water like a storm squall and howled down on him as he clung to the rock, throwing him across Theano and Kenofer below, his cloak strings holding by some miracle but with the heavy stuff wound over eyes and mouth. As he fought to get free of it, to get his breath, he could hear a woman screaming close at hand and the wind still howling. A body moved beneath him; he tried to roll clear, got his head free and gasped for breath.

The air was full of parching ash and the sky that had been almost light was pitch dark. Theano was beside him, clinging to her brother, but Kenofer had his head buried in her tunic and even over the wind Asterion could hear that he was sobbing.

From above them came a high-pitched scream, fading in the darkness as a guard lost his balance in the storm wind and fell from the low tower, rolling away into the blackness at the edge of the cliff.

Theano's mouth was open and she was shouting, but the wind tore away her words; then she pointed to the east. The whole sky above a bank of darkness higher than the horizon was aglow with fire, and higher up lightning played in great sheets. Everything else was black.

It began to rain, large drops at first, then a cloud-burst that drenched them as they huddled together, trying to shelter under their cloaks but not daring to move for fear of being blown away. Somewhere below in the blackness Isander and his men and the people of Minoa sheltered, but for the moment they were the only three in a world of rain and thunder and dark.

Then the rain stopped and only the lightning played on over their heads. Asterion wriggled round and saw that behind to the west the silhouette of the mountains just showed, as if the pall of cloud had broken over the mainland. Then for the first time for many hours there was a time when the thunder ceased and when it came again it was in peals that faded, and there were pauses in between, as there is with ordinary thunder.

Kenofer slowly raised his head and they looked at each other, still speechless, stunned beyond the use of words by what they had heard and seen, aware only of each other's eyes and dirty faces marked by the rain and dust. Theano's soft hair was plastered black against her head, and there was blood on Asterion's bare arms and legs where rocks and thorns had torn him as he fell.

It was Kenofer who broke the silence. "It has come. What I felt for so long, the full meaning of the terror that came to me at the time of the Choosing. The God has done what he willed."

"But what has he done?" cried Theano.

"I don't know. That day, the day of the Choosing was a

time of harvest. Now the God has taken a different harvest, and we still live."

The wind came only in gusts and it was safe to stand up. Asterion wrung out his soaking cloak and began to search for the food and the water-jar. The basket had gone, but when she moved Theano found the bundle of bread scraps where she had been lying. Then Asterion found the jar wedged between two rocks, skimmed with dust but still half full.

They waited, the three who had come safely from the south and had lived through the sending of the God. The light grew stronger, though lightning still danced over the sea to the east. They could hear wailing from the clustered people lower on the rock, where it seemed that some had been hurt, and those of the guard who were left ran down the hillside to join them. They waited on, not knowing what would happen next.

It was hours after what would have been noon on an ordinary day when the sun passed across the sky as it should instead of glowering through a sunset of clouds; they had mostly been sitting with their heads bowed and eyes shut, except that Theano had started to cough. A shout came from the people below and Asterion raised his head and opened his eyes. A group of men were standing and pointing. Far out across the sea where the darkness was deepest there was another darkness, but this was like a great line across the horizon, a darkness that moved, racing toward them.

He stood up, and the others, seeing him move, stood too. Asterion pointed. Already the darkness was nearer, and it seemed that the very shape of the sky had changed. It came towards them faster than anything made by man could travel, not darkness only but a shape and a roaring of sound as if the thunder of Kallisté had broken loose and was coming towards them.

"Quickly, get down." At last Kenofer had found his voice. They crouched below the rocks, clinging together; a wind came howling again from the east, but not louder than the thunder of the darkness which had swept almost to the base of the rock. And then Asterion knew what it was, a wave greater than any he had seen in the worst of his nightmares on the crossing from Kallisté.

It came on, a mountain of water, half as high seemingly as the great rock on which they sheltered. Then he knew why Kenofer's vision had driven them up towards the highest part of Minoa. Here they were safe, above its power . . . but what of the harbour?

The water struck the rock and it trembled, mighty as it was. Spray blew in their faces and the thunder of sound was about them again, and then the crest had passed. Sheltered as they were by the highest part of the rock they did not see it strike the town, only heard a grinding roar that went on and on, and the second shock as the great wall of water fell back, its force broken inland by the lower slopes of the mountains.

The noise faded and the wind began to drop; westwards it grew lighter, but from the people of the harbour another wail went up, hopeless, uncomprehending, the wail of a child when it is frightened and does not understand.

Kenofer said, "If the water comes like that to the Great Island it will sweep Amnissos from the shore and leave it as clean as a plate licked by a beggar."

"And Knossos?"

"The water? I don't know. But if the land shook as it did here the House of the Axe will have gone beyond even Isander's skill to make it again."

"And Phaestos?" whispered Theano. "The mountains to the north are high."

"The fear came to me when I was there. I am certain that the danger has spread even so far, but I cannot guess what new thing the God will do. May we live long enough to know the fate of our friends!" said Kenofer quietly. "Asterion, is it safe to climb up now and see what the water has done?"

Asterion looked at him. The bard's eyelids were swollen and almost closed, so that he was nearly blind, and Theano was coughing again. Shivering in his sodden cloak he climbed the slope behind. At the top Theano saw him stand for a long time, looking first down, then south and north. When he came back his face was blank.

Theano, afraid to go herself, could not bear the look of that face. "Asterion, what did you see?"

"Nothing, there's nothing there. It's like a tablet a scribe has rubbed smooth with his thumb. We're on an island, the harbour isn't there any longer, just some rocks between here and the shore. And that's bare, all the orchards and farms, everything, all gone. Only bare mountains. It's . . ."

And then he crouched down, his head buried in his arms, trying to blot out the sight of that nothing, until he felt Theano's touch, and he who should have been the strong one felt for the first time one small spark of comfort.

18 ⚬ The Eye of a Bird

They stood below the western cliff of the rock. The sun had set in a sky the colour of blood and they had lain for a second night huddled together in the wet bushes waiting for what else the God might send, but there had been nothing more. The thunder had gone, and when the dawn came the sky had lightened towards the east, though that way cloud hung high against the sky. Isander came up through the dripping undergrowth and crouched talking quietly to Kenofer.

At dawn they drank the last of the water—there was nothing to eat—and then began to pick their way down the path and through the encampment of the people of Minoa, Isander's men following them. The misery they found there was even greater than their own, but there was something else as well, a silence and then a knowledge of hate. A woman sheltering under a makeshift tent made from a sail, with two children sprawling across her lap, turned her head and spat as they passed. A voice said "They came from Kallisté!" Theano understood then and quickened her step. They were the bearers of ill-luck, the town was lost for their coming to it out of the east, bringing destruction behind them. That was all that the people of Minoa, those who were left, knew or could bring themselves to understand. If they were not clear of the rock that was now an island before the people shook themselves free from the numbing shock of their loss, then they might yet pay with their lives for what had happened.

She could see that Asterion had understood too. They all quickened their pace, stumbling down a path partly washed away by the rain, and then as it reached the south side they came to the level that the great wave had reached.

Asterion had been right. The rock was licked clean, nothing grew below, there was only wet rock and the restless sea. Above the tide level they picked their way round to the west end of the island and then stood looking across at the land. The new channel was perhaps two spear-casts wide and part way across there was a reef of rock, but it was clear that the water was too deep to wade. One of Isander's men had fallen and cut his head, and his friends were carrying him between them.

Theano guided Kenofer to a place where he could sit and then climbed down after Asterion to the water's edge.

Now that they could see more clearly, the far shore was littered with wreckage, smashed boats, the roof-beams of houses, trees torn up by their roots. Crouching beside him Theano asked, "Can you swim?"

"A little, not far enough."

She shaded her eyes; the light was quite good now. "There, no, farther down by the red rock, it looks like a raft."

Asterion followed where she pointed. "I think it's part of a flat roof."

"Would it float?"

"If we could get to it, but I couldn't manage it alone."

"Wait then."

While Theano climbed back to the others, Asterion looked down at the rocks immediately below; there was wreckage washed up there too. By the time Theano came back with Isander and one of his men he had found part of a door he could cling to. Isander said nothing; he looked across at the broken water and then back at Kenofer and the injured man, and waded into the sea.

Theano, her hands to her mouth, watched them go. Isander

was kicking out strongly, but once she saw Asterion go under, his head lost in a flurry of foam as a wave broke over him. He came up again, the planks bobbing ahead of him. Beyond the rocks she lost them again until they pulled themselves out on the other side.

After they had manhandled the makeshift raft down to the water's edge she climbed up for a second time to help Kenofer down to the water. He had been waiting quietly, sitting where she had put him, as if he was an old man. He was very tired, for the thunderings and terrors of the day before seemed to have sucked the life from him and left him too weary even to sleep. Between his swollen eyelids he could now see only a blur of light or darkness, and though the pain from them was not severe it was insistent. Yet in his heart there was a quietness, so that he was content to do what Theano thought best for him. The moment would soon come to step clear of the tide race that had carried him for so long, and then there would be time to rest, even if peace was longer in coming.

Afterwards they were none of them sure how it had been done. Theano remembered things in fits and starts. Kenofer's blind eyes raised to the spray, calm even when the raft bucked in the current, Asterion, his bare body streaming with water, paddling furiously as he sat astride a beam, the hurt man's white face. They grounded far down the bay where the waves had swept them, and nearly at the shore Asterion had lost his balance and almost drowned. After Isander had pumped the water out of him he lay spent in the dryer sand clear of the waves, his mouth parched with salt.

He was hungry too, but there was still nothing to eat. There would be nothing for any of them until they had climbed inland towards the mountains, above the level of the ruin left by the wave. The people of Minoa faced starvation as well, but they had some store of food on the rock.

Asterion dragged himself up on his elbow, got a knee under his body and then stood, holding weakly to Theano while his head span and settled. She brushed the caked sand from him.

"Hold on to this." It was a stick from the wreckage above the water line.

Isander took one arm of the injured man, and Theano went to Kenofer, who put his hand upon her shoulder. Together they led the others back along the shore. The mountains were high behind where the harbour had been; they were kept close to the water line until they were well past and a low headland hid the rock from them; no one turned back to see it disappear from sight. Far inland they could see at the head of a shallow valley the golden sheen of barley fields too high up to have been reached by the flood. The lower part of the track which led that way was lost, and they stumbled between rolled boulders on ground like a dry river-bed, between the stumps of a ruined olive-grove. Once they passed a dead goat caught in the upper branches of a tree, but it was already stinking and the crows had been at it; then gradually the ruin grew less.

It was long after midday that the goatherds found them. Asterion had dropped far behind, but the others had gathered under the shelter of the first tree that still bore its leaves. They could not see the sea now and the sun was hot through a thin veil of cloud. Theano saw that Kenofer's lips were cracked and ran her tongue across her own.

The men who came down the slope towards them were rough-haired and burnt almost black by the sun. A boy carried a kid under his arm and the mother ran behind.

One man went back down the track to help Asterion to the shelter of the tree. Then they passed round their water-bottles and while the goat was milked into a cup began to ask questions.

Some words were the same, but their accents were so strange that Theano could make almost nothing of what they were saying. Then Kenofer raised his head and spoke in what seemed to be a language she had never heard him use before. Through all that had happened the leather lyre-case still hung from his shoulder, the only thing saved from the island. Kenofer fumbled blindly for the fastenings and Theano took it from him and opened it. The lyre was almost whole; one of the curved birds' heads had split and a string had gone, but the others were dry and it would play again.

One of the goatherds put out a hand knotted as a tree root and touched it, and the strings woke and hummed.

"They know who I am," Kenofer said. "I came this way three years back and they remember. They are pretty much their own men on this side of the mountains, but there is the house of a king beyond at Sparta, about as far as Phaestos is from Knossos. I think these men will care for us until we are strong enough to go so far. At least, although I can hardly see, I still have something with which to repay them," and he laid his hand on the lyre.

Then he reached deeper into the bottom of the leather bag and brought out a package wrapped in rags. "Is it still whole?" He handed it to Theano, who unwrapped it carefully.

In her hand lay the fragment of plaster from Kallisté, with the keen eye of the bird painted more than a generation before and yet still bright.

They rested until the heat of the afternoon was over and then followed the shepherds to their village. Theano and Asterion walked together. For the first time since the God had broken Kallisté they were quiet and there was certainty of what would happen next.

Asterion looked ahead at Kenofer, being led up the rough path by one of the men. "Did he plan all the time that we would come here?" he asked.

"No, how could he? He didn't know which way the wind would blow. He has just taken one step forward at a time; but he has been to Achaea before. I remember it was the last time that the Master left the island, he took Kenofer with him. It was as if he were showing him the places he would one day need to know. They were away a whole summer, and by the time the Master came back he was ill and he has hardly played since."

"So Kenofer is sure of his welcome, a bard can find a home anywhere," said Asterion bitterly. "I was sent north away from my people who may now be in great need. We've seen the destruction of Minoa—what has the God brought to Phaestos and my father? Do you think that across the mountains I can find a boat going south? Surely the omen has been fulfilled now?"

Theano caught her breath, suddenly cold and weak inside; yet why should Asterion stay with them, what was there to keep him, if he could go home? She looked at Kenofer, the master of persuasion, walking ahead, and wondered what he would say, and then it seemed that the words were given her.

"I think it wasn't only Kenofer who was guided every step of the way, but all of us. All for a reason. Think of your father now; he may be in great hardship but perhaps his one hopeful thought is that you may be safe, far away before the disaster struck. It was his wish that you should come with us. You may have to wait some time before there is any hope of sailing south and finding him. Will you wait with us? I'm sorry, I know it will be hard for you."

Then Asterion stopped and turned towards her and took her by the elbows, looking down at her with a face that was marked with tears.

"Hard? But after all, you are here!"

It was ten days more before they came down the west side of the mountains, through a fold in the foothills, to a wide plain even more beautiful than Phaestos, but bounded by mountains that lay a different way, north and south. The shepherds had cared for them well, and they had rested in their village while the hurt man recovered and Kenofer's swollen eyes grew less sore and Theano's cough eased. But the dust of Kallisté still seemed to blow in the wind although the sun shone more clearly as the days passed, and it would take longer than a few days to restore any of them to full health.

To Theano now it seemed that they had been travelling ever since she was a child, and indeed in half a month what had happened to her and Asterion had changed them into a man and a woman, but she knew that they could not go much further. Kenofer's eyes needed the skill of a healer, and they were all gaunt and burned by the sun. There must soon be a settled place, a home where she could lie down and sleep knowing that the next night would be the same and the one after. She had always understood that she was not one to wander far. She needed to know the shape of the mountains that guarded her home in the darkness. Now as they walked new mountains were rising, higher than any she had seen so close before, a great wall down the western side of the broad valley, with dark knees like the foothills of Ida, cleft by ravines and with snow still among the peaks at midsummer. She asked Kenofer their name.

He turned his clouded eyes as if searching for them against the clear blue of the sky. "Taygetos. We have come to the kingdom of the king of Sparta. He is an old man but I have played for him before."

The shepherds had passed them from one guide to another across the eastern mountains; now they were on a broad way leading north to Sparta itself. It still seemed a long road to the foot of the mountains. Theano could not walk far at a time and they went slowly, resting where there was shade. It was late in the morning of the day when they reached the road that Theano saw dust ahead, the sign of someone moving fast, and then heard the thunder of chariot wheels.

She turned, catching Kenofer by the arm to drag him out of the way, but the chariots, three of them, stopped short in a skitter of stones, plunging horses and shouts from the drivers. A tall young man with fair hair flying, dressed in short wide leather breeches in a style Theano had never seen before, jumped down from the leading chariot and strode towards them. Then he stood, smiling easily, staring from one to the other, and she realised that they looked no more than beggars.

"Is it the bard from Kallisté?"

Kenofer's head went up, and the young man noticed his swollen eyes. "Oh my lord, forgive me, I did not know you, but it was more than two years ago when we met last. We had word that you were in the mountains and my father grew impatient and sent me to find you. We did not know that you were in such need."

They were expected. News can travel faster than a bird flies even through barren country, and now they were known and waited for. Theano felt tears prick behind her eyes.

The young prince took in the situation with a practised glance. "I will leave some of my men with you to guide your companions to a farm where they can wait for litters. My lord, will the road be too rough for you in my chariot?"

"Not if my sister comes with us to guide me at the other end. I would not wish to mistake the person of the king in his own hall. And Asterion, son of Prince Geryon of Phaestos."

The prince had a cheerful laugh. "So be it. You shall ride with me, and there is room for the lady and your other companion with my friends."

So for the second time Theano came to a strange palace riding in a chariot, but the house of Cretheus of Sparta was very different from any palace that she had seen in the Great Island. It seemed more like a manor, like Myrtissos with its wide courtyard and the wooden gate and pillars painted and carved. There were the sounds of a farm and stables close by and the servants and women of the house had open friendly faces, not painted as the courtiers of Phaestos had been. Even their clothes were different, simple brightly coloured tunics. They were led through the outer courtyard and portico to the king's hall, where a fire smouldered even at midsummer on a

187

low hearth between the four pillars which supported the roof. The king was an old man in a long robe, seated near the hearth in a high-backed chair, but he rose to greet the bard as Theano led Kenofer through the doorway.

And now, as he stood in a tattered shepherd's kilt, his hair tied back with a leather thong, Kenofer still had about him the dignity that he had worn when he had sung in his embroidered robe in the halls of other kings. The God had taken much from him in return for his gift, but he had not taken that.

The fair-haired wife of the king's eldest son, the one who had ridden to meet them, came through from the women's rooms and took Theano away. She turned back, suddenly afraid that her brother would need her and frightened to be alone with this strange princess who spoke her language in an unfamiliar way.

"No, be easy," said the young woman. "He will be tended well. It is time you were cared for too, coming from beneath the thunder of Kallisté as you do."

While she stood shyly in the women's hall servants were sent running for warm water and a dress to fit Theano, and then the princess turned her to the light.

"Oh, but you are pretty! When we have washed your hair and smoothed your skin all the young men will be looking at you. But that other, the dark young man, is he your brother too or your husband?"

When she saw from Theano's blushing that he was neither, she laughed and kissed her for the first time.

That night Theano slept in a clean bed under a clean cover, in a room with other girls who were gentle with her as Aethra had once been when she woke crying in the night, dreaming again of the terror of thunder and darkness. The next morning they led her back to the men's hall and she found Kenofer sitting comfortably near the king with Asterion in attendance, unfamiliar in the dress of the country but still looking the prince he was. Kenofer stretched out his hands to her and she knelt beside him.

"Theano, when you agreed to come with me I promised you journeyings, but it seems that there will be only one, though that harder than I had ever dreamed. Will you stay with me here?" And Theano had no words, but she put her hands over his.

19 ❦ The Third Friend

Theano was sitting on the floor of the women's hall in the palace of Sparta. She had been helping to sort the wool that would be needed for setting up the loom. The day before they had cut loose the great web of a cloak with a border of small stiff-legged horses that they had been working on since mid-winter. Now it was spring and she sat with a ball of wool in her hands staring at nothing, not seeing the princess's look of concern or hearing the chatter of the other girls.

It had been so long now. During the first months in Sparta, while they were recovering from the ordeal of the rock and of their journeyings, it had been enough to wake in the peace and comfort of the women's rooms and know that the day would pass with no greater excitement than the baby prince cutting a new tooth. It had been a long time before Kenofer had begun to move and smile again as a young man does; his sight, which had faded quickly during their travelling, had never returned and now he was almost blind. On their first day in Sparta he had told her that this would now be their home, and after all that had happened she would have been content, except for Asterion.

She had not seen him for ten, no, eleven days now. As soon as the winter storms were over and there was a chance of boats coming from the south he had got leave to go down to the harbour on the coast and wait for what news might come from the Great Island. In the long months since the end of Kallisté they had heard little, but it had all been horrible. Isander had sailed at the beginning of autumn, as soon as he could find anyone to take him through the stormy waters with their reefs of floating pumice and the dust clouds that still hung in the sky and made the sunsets terrible as a palace on fire. He had not come back, but he had promised to send news, and if he had lived through the crossing he would keep his word. At the time Asterion had been certain that he should not yet return to Phaestos—the working out of both his own fate and that of the court he had left behind had been too uncertain—but during the winter he had fretted and grown more and more silent.

"Theano?" The princess who had so quickly become her friend touched her shoulder to rouse her. She pointed to the doorway.

Kenofer stood there, waiting for her to guide him across the floor littered with wool and children's toys to the seat in the west-facing porch. He liked to sit there and feel the sun warm on his cheek as it hung above the high peaks of Taygetos, casting deep blue and purple shadows across the greenness of a plain he could no longer see. As she jumped up to go to him she saw that he was carrying his lyre, and that was good, for sometimes days would pass when his hands lay still in his lap and it seemed as if he had been robbed of not one sense but two. There could be no real peace for any of them yet, knowing that while they sat calm beyond the storm the world they had known had been shattered. It seemed that the God of Kallisté had laid the Great Island in ruins as surely as he had destroyed Minoa beneath the rock.

Kenofer sat down and settled the lyre into the curve of his arm. "What shall I play?" he asked the girls who had clustered round him. They knew now not to ask for the lament for Kallisté.

"The shepherd's song," said one.

"Please, Kenofer, the laughing one, the song you made for Theano when she was small." That was the princess's favourite.

He touched the strings lightly and the dancing music of children playing floated out so that the serving women carrying water beyond in the courtyard stopped to listen. The fairhaired girls in their bright dresses sat quietly, but the princess's baby, who had been carried in in the arms of his nurse, chuckled and shouted because he loved music.

Kenofer heard him. "Is that my lord the prince?"

"Who else would shout when a famous bard is playing?" said his mother, carrying him over to the group in the porch. "He has no manners!"

"May I hold him?"

Theano bent forward and took the lyre as the princess put the heavy baby into his arms. The child bounced and crowed, trying to grasp the long dark locks that Kenofer still wore after the fashion of Kallisté. He was warm and sweet-smelling and very full of life, his hair a cap of soft fair silk under Kenofer's hand.

The child grabbed for his nose and Kenofer held him high, giggling; then he turned back to the princess.

"Here is your son, lady. I am sure he is as beautiful as he is noisy. Now I have a gift for you if he will let me play in peace."

It was a long time since he had felt like this, he thought, as he took the lyre back from Theano and tuned it before a respectful and hushed audience. In all the months in Sparta he had made nothing new which had pleased him enough to be worth remembering. Now a feeling like a voice one has almost forgotten was stirring again, and he knew whose voice it was.

As he began to sing the princess felt Theano's hand slip into hers and clutch tightly, and she put her arm round the younger girl's shoulders, not fully understanding but seeing tears on Theano's cheeks and realising for the first time why men praised the bard from Kallisté so highly.

Then there were tears on her own cheeks, for it was a song

for a baby, her baby, though not a lullaby. The little prince was strong and lively and it was that hopeful new beginning that Kenofer sang of, seeing in his mind spring on the cold heights, when the first new green things push through brown leaves and frozen earth. And as so often in his songs there was a chorus that could be sung by anyone, when they had heard it once, and soon all the girls were humming and dancing the baby on his soft bare feet in time to the song.

A man's voice, abrupt and harsh through the music, sounded outside the women's hall. Theano, her hand still holding that of the princess, did not know that she had gripped her till it hurt. Among a thousand voices she would know Asterion's.

The guard at the doorway looked through as if searching for someone. Asterion did not follow him. Then Theano picked up her long skirts and ran out into the courtyard outside. He was standing there, in a short tunic like those the men of Sparta wore for riding, still caked from the dusty roads, his hair uncombed and his boots splashed from fords deep with spring rain, and behind him was Isander.

Their love was acknowledged now and she could go into his arms with no thought of who might see.

"Theano!" He said no more than her name and then put his head down on her shoulder, tall as he was, so that she could see the thin grim face of Isander.

"You've come back." It was a stupid way to greet him, but Isander nodded gravely in answer.

"I was sent. There were . . . are things that must be told to you all."

Then the princess followed Theano out into the courtyard, saw the weary men and began to arrange the welcome of her guests.

Theano led Asterion away towards the men's rooms; he held her hand but still said nothing. In the doorway where she must leave him he turned and looked down at her as if about to speak, but then seemed to change his mind.

"No, let Isander tell you all together."

What she saw in his eyes was worse than a wound, worse even than Kenofer's blindness. The same blank suffering that had been there on the morning of the omen of the horn.

Kenofer could still walk freely through the familiar rooms of the palace, so she did not hear him come up behind her. He took Asterion and hugged him.

"Good, you're home, and I have a new song. There's time for a bath before the evening meal and you smell as if you need one."

He had not seen what was in Asterion's face, but Theano knew that he had been aware of it. Yet the look he gave her as the two young men went down the passage together was unexpectedly reassuring. Theano was no longer a little girl to believe that her brother could make everything right, but she felt comforted.

The evening meal in the great hall of Sparta was always noisy with the king's barons, the young men of his guard, visitors and travellers, crowding together to eat the good meat that came from the pastures and high valleys, and to laugh with the maids who served it. Yet tonight about the king and his family and the four who had come from the Great Island there was a small space of quiet, and the princess signed to her housekeeper that the sideboards were to be cleared early and the wine-drinking not prolonged.

Then the old king spoke. "It is hard to ask the bearer of ill news to speak his message, but waiting will make it no easier. Isander, will you tell us what you have seen?"

Isander looked at the circle of grave faces, the old king, the prince his son with his young wife, trying to understand the sorrow of those who were now their friends, and the three from Phaestos. Theano sat on the floor, leaning against Kenofer's knee; the bard's hands were quiet in the lap of his singing robe and his lyre stood untouched on the floor beside him. Asterion, who had hardly spoken or eaten, sat a little apart, still twisting the stem of an empty wine goblet in his hands, tracing and retracing the shape of an octopus that was painted on it.

"I can't be sure what you've heard. I've been away so long."

"Only a little here and a little there, like the news men shout when they run from a fire. We know that the House of the Axe fell in the earthshaking, and that Amnissos and the north coast were scoured by waves as high as a tower," said the prince.

"There was a tale that a boat from Pylos had been blown eastward by a storm and had passed Milos, but where Kallisté should have been there was only a pillar of smoke and steam rising from the middle of a ring of rock, like the broken off rim of a jug. But could that be so? The men of Pylos are given to tall stories." The old king's voice was doubtful.

"This time they spoke true. But had you no word of Phaestos?" asked Isander.

"Nothing but a tale of death under a white dust that we found hard to believe," said Kenofer.

"If you had spent a month choking in the same dust on Kallisté you would not have found it so strange," said Isander. "My friends, the gods dealt differently with each of the great houses of the island, and the doom that came to Phaestos was the most difficult to understand."

Then he stopped again, as if not yet able to speak what must be told.

"What did you find when you reached the Great Island?" Kenofer asked gently.

"You know how the sea was, floating with pumice and driftwood; a storm hit us two days south of harbour and I thought when we made landfall we were far out of our way, for I could recognise nothing. There was cloud over the island, low on the mountains as if they still smoked as Kallisté did, and that made me afraid. Then it lifted and I saw the Warrior, the lone mountain behind Knossos. It was already a month since the sending of the gods. I thought it would be as it had been before after other earthshakings, buildings thrown down but already the scaffolding growing to raise them again, and men working in the fields to sow what seed had been saved. This time there was nothing. It was all still . . . broken. Kenofer, you saw Kallisté, you know, but this was worse."

"There were no people, no cattle?" asked the old king.

"Not a beast, not a growing thing except the stumps of trees, until we had forced our way inland to Knossos. There there were a few, sheltering in caves, some of the king's guard standing watch over the ruins of the palace. But no king, no court. We went south to Phaestos then, but we knew before we saw the plain what we would find, because there had been signs of it even in the high valleys of Ida. It was as well that we carried our own food, for there was hardly a blade of grass on the earth or bird in the air."

"Then you came to the pass above Phaestos and what did you see?" asked Kenofer, remembering the road so well and the many times after the first when he had stood and looked down at the green plain where those he loved would welcome him. In spite of all the rumours that had come north he still held it so, a bright quiet picture in his mind, for those were the only pictures he could see. And now it was not there, would never be there again, even if the God gave him back his eyes. He put a hand down to Theano and she took it in both of hers.

"We saw death," said Isander. "A quiet death, perhaps, but almost more cruel than the riven earth and fallen hillsides of Knossos. The dust blown from Kallisté had come down over the whole plain, little and little, breaking roofs with the weight of it, sifting into wells, filling the ruins as deep as the height of a man. It had buried the vines and stripped the olives of every leaf and then of their branches. It will be a generation before anything can grow there again."

"All the plain, everywhere?" asked Theano through her tears. Not Myrtissos, not Myrtissos as well.

"We did not go down far. We took the path west above the foothills of Ida, the way that leads to the high cave of the Mistress, and I believe that we were guided to take that way, for on the third day we found them. Those who were alive."

"He found my father," said Asterion and Kenofer felt such a surge of relief that the tears started in his eyes and he heard himself gasp as if he had been struck.

"He was still alive . . . then," said Asterion.

Frozen, speechless, but with the tears that had begun in joy still running down his cheeks, Kenofer heard Isander to the end.

The earthshaking and the darkness had come even as far south as Phaestos, the palace had fallen and the king and queen been killed under it, but Geryon had taken the Summer Guard and those able-bodied men who would follow his lead and had begun to marshall the people to safety on the higher ground west of the plain, sheltered by the mountains from the worst of the dust. There had been many who would not come, and many too weak, and some had died on the journey, but thousands had climbed up into the mountains where there was still water though very little food. And behind them their homes and their farms had been buried, stifled by the relentless rain of dust.

Then the prince had sent scouts ahead and had found that not far along the coast there were places that the devastation had not touched. To the north and east everything had been destroyed, but in the thickly wooded valleys of the west of the Great Island there was the hope of a new beginning. Isander had gone with them, climbing through the gloom of the dust clouds that still hung above the island. They had come at last to a place where a new city might be built, and Isander had helped Geryon lay it out and seen the first tents and huts go up. For a long time Geryon had seemed to labour alone for the good of the people, but as the days passed others among the lords and captains who still lived seemed to wake from the daze that had numbed them all, and had begun to play their part.

"It was then, when there was the beginning of hope that the people might come through the winter alive, that it happened," said Isander, turning to Kenofer. "The prince had been high on the mountain all day directing the teams who were cutting timber for the first houses. He came down at dusk, and we stood looking between the huts to the glow of the first cooking fires. The children were starting to play again, and the men had at least some shelter to go home to, even if it was only of wattle and mud. He had a cup in his hand that someone had brought him, and I remember he was smiling and I thought it was a long time since I had seen that.

" 'Well, it's a beginning,' he said. Then he dropped the cup and looked at me in a puzzled way and slid down at my feet, as a cloak falls from the back of a chair. When I knelt to turn him over he was already dead, but the smile had not quite left his face."

Asterion stood up and pushed his stool back, so that it fell with a clatter and the servants clearing away at the far end of the hall turned to stare. Without a word he walked quickly out through the portico to the spring night outside.

Theano raised herself as if to follow him.

"No." Kenofer's hand was on her shoulder. "Not yet."

The tall lamps made a soft haze of light against which dark shadows moved. He turned himself towards the voice of Isander. There was a stillness inside his head so that his own voice came from a great distance, but he was calm and he knew the things that he must do, in order, and that he would have the strength to accomplish them. The breath of the God whom he now began to understand stirred in him.

"My friend," he said, "the bringing of that news has cost

you dear. We have a debt to you that we can never repay. But what will you do now?"

"I must go back. I came seeking for what help I can get from the Lords of Achaea, but I must go back to those who are left."

There would be time later to learn in detail who had lived and who had died, the people of Myrtissos and the court, but there was one name more that he must speak, though he did not know how to do it.

Then Theano at his feet asked in her small clear voice, "And the people from the House of Singing Birds? The Master was not an old man, but he was sick."

"When I left the new city he still lived. His pupils made a litter and carried him up through the mountains, and sang as they went. It was their singing and the willing feet and strong shoulders of the Summer Guard that the prince used to get the people through. And they sang too, the Summer Guard, their song of thunder. It has become the song of all the people of Phaestos now, not only of the young men."

Kenofer stood up and Theano with him, so that his hand rested on her shoulder as it did when they went an unfamiliar way.

"Yes, you must go to your friend now," said the old king.

Theano had known where Asterion would be. There was a place on the wall not far from the main gate where a corner turned south; he had gone there before when he had needed peace after the noisy life of the men's courts. As she guided Kenofer to the foot of the steps that led up to the guard's walk she saw his head dark against a sky already lit by a rising moon.

Asterion turned as Kenofer climbed carefully up the last of the steps. Theano could not see his face, for his back was to the eastern mountains, but she had no need to.

"I must go back with Isander," he said. "My father died for the people of Phaestos, my place is still with the Guard. The omen has been fulfilled now."

"You must act as your heart guides you," said Kenofer. "But first listen to a word from your father. Yes, this is what I was to say to you if this moment came."

Asterion drew in his breath through his teeth but did not speak.

"You remember that last day, the day of the omen; as we rode up to the pass we stopped to rest the horses?" It was clear in his own mind, as every detail was of that day; could he make the boy see it? His future and the happiness of Theano depended on it. "It was the only time after we had stood together before the priestess that there was a moment for me to talk to Geryon. Let me try to use his own words. We had spoken of my sending and of the seemingly senseless doom which had struck you down. He said 'What is there behind this, Kenofer? There is a pattern weaving here that I can't understand, do you?' And I told him that I could not see clearly, but that I was sure the pattern was there for us to find. It had not been chance that I had been born on Kalliste, or that the God had given me his gift, or that I had found Phaestos as my second home and him for my friend."

Kenofer paused but Asterion still did not speak. He felt Theano draw loose from his hand and go to the young man.

"Then your father said, 'So, cruel as it may seem, there may be meaning in the fate of my son and the omen that is sending him north with you. Is it from danger or into danger, I wonder? I think Kalliste is the heart of the storm and you will find no peace there and no kind word from the Mistress.' "

"But if we had not gone north to Kalliste, dangerous as it was, we should have been in Phaestos for an even greater danger. So going north was safe for us, as if the God still had work for us to do." Theano felt as if the voice speaking was not fully her own, as if she too had felt a breathing from Kenofer's God. But surely this must have been how it was?

"That was what Geryon said. I remember he turned to me and said, 'Bard, you can twist your omens to mean what you will. Below in the grove your words saved my son, but what if the doom was truly for Phaestos after all, if an end is really coming to all that we know, as I have sometimes dreamed myself?'

" 'What would you want then for your son, if you were the true prophet and not I?' I asked him."

" 'That he should follow what light there was forward, even though it was into the eye of the storm. I would not want him to turn back. If the hand of the Mistress is set against our land then I would want him far from it, for your God in spite of all his thunderings is a kinder God than She.' "

"My father said that, truly?" Asterion's arm was around Theano's shoulders, and she felt it tighten and his back grow straight as if he had let slip a heavy weight.

"As his friend then and your friend now I think he would have you prosper in Sparta. Remember, before he died Isander had brought him word that you were alive, and where, and that must have been a comfort to him; and he did not send word for you to come back. With him gone you might still not be welcome among your own people, and who knows what deeds the God has prepared for you here?"

"That first morning when I met you at the shrine, before Kenofer came, a bird shot up from the track behind you and flew north," said Theano. "I thought then that a god had sent it but I didn't see what it meant. But it seems that it was for all of us."

"Kenofer was saved alive for the power he has in his hands and his voice. What is there that I have brought safe from the Great Island that I should be saved?"

"Yourself," said Kenofer. "You are your father's son, as I know you will never forget. The ways here are different, but as you become a trusted follower of the king there will be much of the wisdom of the Great Island that you will remember when it is needed. Things that as yet you hardly know that you know."

"And me?" asked Theano in a small voice, although already her heart was singing within her.

"You, why you? Because you are yourself and we both need you to look after us! Kenofer, let me go first down the steps." Asterion had his voice under control now.

They went back together into the lighted hall, Theano walking between the two men and holding their hands. At the central fireplace they stopped and Asterion went forward alone and knelt to the king. He spoke no word, but the old man bent forward and took the young man's hands between his old veined fingers in the ancient act of accepting fealty.

A new song was flooding Kenofer's mind. He knew he would sleep little that night, with the new griefs and new hopes that filled him and the music he must make from both of them. He had never made Geryon his own song for Phaestos, never while he was alive to hear it, but he could make it now. In each of those two places where he had been happy a friend had died, and after Phormio he had made the lament for Kallisté. Then his life had run in deeper channels and of his friendship with Geryon he knew that the God would also make something worthy. And now there was Asterion, who would soon be his brother, and his third friend; the first song he had made for him had been a song of thunder, but now there must be a marriage song.

Outside in the moonlit night a wind blew down from the mountains to sing in the rafters of the high hall of Sparta, but there was no thunder. They would only hear that now when it came at the proper time of the summer rain. Asterion had come back to stand at Theano's side and he heard her make the small pleased sound that comes with a good idea.

"What is it?"

"So often Kenofer has talked about a pattern he could not properly see. I suddenly thought about weaving. We were setting up a loom at Myrtissos when my brother found me alive again. I want to set up a loom again myself now to make you a cloak, mostly dark—our pattern has been dark, but with a bright border."

"How will you weave that, Theano?" asked Kenofer, who had heard what she said.

"With birds, like the ones Father painted on the wall at home, like the one we found. Birds with bright eyes, that have flown safe through the eye of a storm."

Author's Note

We are frightened by what we do not understand and feel we cannot control. When we are small it may be by the life-sized teddy which was chosen lovingly as a birthday present but which terrifies us, or only by rain on the window. I remember being scared of a factory hooter that used to sound at night from the other side of the town; I thought that was when they let out the wild bulls and my father would be trampled if he was out then! But people have always tried to find explanations for the unknown, and before science gave us some of the answers they made their gods to fit the evidence.

Most early people have had a mother goddess, a symbol of fertility, and when a merchant from one land found the cult of a goddess in a temple near a strange harbour he was generally glad to worship her as someone familiar but with a different name. The twelve gods of Olympus of whom we read in Homer are only the end product, the survivors, of many gods who were worshipped in mainland Greece and across the islands to Crete during the centuries before. Hera and Athena and Aphrodite are the descendants of the Mistress, worshipped in Minoan Crete, and of other goddesses with unfamiliar names like Akakallis and Britomartis who had mountain shrines and sacred groves all across the island. The male gods of Crete were more shadowy; the Cretans knew a Zeus, although he was younger than Olympian Zeus, and rather different. The Mistress had various sons and consorts, but no one who would correspond exactly to Apollo. Yet men were already feeling towards the idea of such a God, and this is what Kenofer is doing in this book. It would have been men like him who were drawing closer to the idea of a God who would be the source of all creative inspiration and yet could strike as swiftly as an arrow in flight against what displeased him.

Exceptional creative power has always been a mystery which cannot be explained away entirely by heredity or training, so it was reasonable to ascribe it to the intervention of a God. This did not make it any easier for someone like Kenofer who was blessed with it than it has been for artists and musicians down the centuries. I have also made Kenofer 'earthquake-sensitive'; this is a rare and unexplained gift, but I have met someone who had it and always felt ill before an earthquake occurred, even if it happened many miles away.

The other theme of the book was a most horrifying and concrete reality to those who lived through it. The volcanic eruption of the small island of Santorini in the middle of the Aegean Sea is thought to have been the largest in historic times, up to four times as powerful as the eruption of Krakatoa in 1883. It blew the whole centre out of the island, rained volcanic ash and pumice over the eastern end of the Mediterranean and engulfed much of the north coast of Crete, a hundred kilometres away, in tidal waves. My characters watched the eruption from Monemvassia on the eastern coast of the Peloponnese and only just escaped with their lives. The destruction was colossal and is thought to have brought about such political chaos in the eastern half of the island that the way was left open for Mycenaean and later Dorian invaders from the mainland of Greece; perhaps some very distant descendants of Theano went with them. The effect it may have had on the lives of individuals I have tried to imagine.

It is relatively easy to set a book in the later classical period, where we have a written literature and a vast amount of other material to tell us how people lived. But Santorini probably erupted somewhere near 1450 B.C. and so far back there are big gaps in our knowledge. The palaces of Crete we know, what the people looked like who lived in them, but not exactly how they lived; however, they would have been a southern people, more excitable and demonstrative than we are in northern Europe. The only real inventions in the book are the idea of the Summer Guard and the Choosing at Phaestos.

The idea of the Summer Guard came from two places. The first is an account of a very similar event which was part of the rite of manhood for the Dorians who were living in Crete some centuries later; such customs often persist for a very long time. The other source is the wall paintings at Knossos, where handsome boys and young men, beautifully dressed, are shown bearing gifts to the king, and occupied in dancing and religious festivals. They must have had a special function, just as the pages and squires in a mediaeval palace were part of a well-organised system.

If anyone is particularly interested in the eruption at Santorini, a paperback called *The End of Atlantis* by Professor J. V. Luce reads more like a detective story than a historical and geological investigation—which it really is. Excavations have been going on recently in Santorini which may well prove my guesses about what the town looked like to be quite wrong, but one can only go on what is available.